One

truth [trooth]

the formless, indefinable and untouchable essence whose nature is inherent joy that is not of this world

TheHamsterWheelIsNotMotorized.com

Twenty-two

myth [mith]

an invalid collective or individual belief or experience
that is used to project a seeming reality

Thank you

Thank you to my wife Narmada for inspiring me to write and expressing the dance of life in its most sublime form.

Thank you to Paul Hedderman at zenbitchslap.com for generously sharing his invitation and for inspiring me with ideas for the book title, insights and stories.

Thank you to everyone reading this
– and everyone not reading this.

aum

Benjamin Ramakrishna

THE HAMSTER WHEEL IS NOT MOTORIZED

BUSTING 22 MYTHS THAT SEEMINGLY RESTRAIN US FROM BEING FULLY ALIVE

Get in touch with the author: benjamin@thehamsterwheelisnotmotorized.com

Visit TheHamsterWheelIsNotMotorized.com

Published in Germany in October 2016
by ekabhava publishing | Benjamin Schmid| Schlüterstr. 14 | 20146 Hamburg
publishing@ekabhava.org
Cover design by Tanya Gupta
Illustrations by Rohini Ramaprasad

ISBN: 978-3-9818178-0-5

0

You are full of life

1

You already are what you are looking for

2

You are invincible

3

The world is in you

4

You are good enough by nature

5

The outside is a reflection of your inside

6

You are happy – whether with or without your partner

O

You are full of life

PREFACE

The best way to get out of something
is to realize you were never in it.
– Paul Hedderman

Imagine you are dreaming, and in the dream, you are cheating on your boyfriend or girlfriend, which leaves a very unpleasant aftertaste. You feel extremely guilty and cannot comprehend how you could have done what you did to someone who really means something to you. You are immensely worried and confused about whether you should tell your boyfriend or girlfriend and whether he or she would find out about it. You are becoming more and more worried and hopeless and do not see any way out of this difficult situation.

Suddenly, you wake up realizing that all of it was just a dream. What seemed to be an unbearable problem during the dream – from the perspective of the person in the dream, which you identified with, and hence, felt as real as it can get for you – no longer represents a dilemma for you in the waking state. It is not only that the problem disappeared, but also that it never even existed in the first place. You did not solve the situation by using a conventional method, such as finding a compromise, going to therapy or learning how to think positively, but by realizing you were never the person in the dream. As soon as the identification dropped, the problem was gone. The person in the dream would have never been able to solve the issue with the same quality as you did by waking up; neither through any method nor any meditation practice. At best, you could have slightly improved the situation or learned how to cope with it, but it would have always been a burden in your life in some way or another. You cannot truly sort out an issue by looking at it from the same perspective that caused it initially. Put differently, the problem was not derived from cheating on your boyfriend or girlfriend, but from identifying with something that is different from your true nature, that is the *dream-constructed* person.

This dream analogy points out that, in everyday life, the vast majority of us are disoriented and seemingly lost because we have forgotten that we are not in the dream, but the one dreaming. It is essential to understand that we can only seemingly be in the dream, but never in actuality. While to the person in the dream everything within it appears to be real, it can never be real to the one who is awake. I was seemingly stuck in the dream for a long time myself without even having the slightest idea of its mechanism. I was so immersed in the dream trying to look for long-lasting remedy always *banging my head against a brick wall,* not seeing that who or what we are is never to be found within the dream.

Although so-called personal development or self-improvement methods can have a positive effect on us, they require effort, discipline and repetition and their efficacy is very limited because they work within the dream. They mainly numb or reposition symptoms, but do not enable us to see our true identity. Instead, they even reinforce the seeming reality of the dream by keeping us within that very realm. We can only find a long-lasting cure-all for the events happening in the dream when being awake. As the person within the dream, we can never understand how it feels to be awake.

This book is an invitation to be open-minded to the possibility that we may not be who we think we are. Life does not have to be an ongoing struggle for survival or fight for acceptance and love. It is possible to live a light-hearted life and be successful without having to worry or be greedy. Life is very simple: no matter what happens, it is always enough to be ourselves.

Therefore, this book is not about learning yet another method or set of beliefs, but about challenging the status quo and discovering together whether it is possible to be completely free – and not just a little. While we may experience a temporary relief when trying to be free as the person within the dream, we experience ongoing freedom when realizing that we have never been in the dream in the first place. All chapters of this book are about discovering our inherent nature using different everyday situations as a starting point.

HOW TO READ THIS BOOK

Each chapter consists of two parts. The first part describes *what we believe or seemingly experience to be true*. Or put in other words, it describes 22 myths about how we usually experience life, especially when conforming or being *well-adjusted* to society in terms of what we should think, what values we should have and how we should see the world. It takes the representative perspective of someone who acts upon the common belief system that we acquire through our upbringing in society. That first part does not represent the perspective of the author.

The words *believe* and *seeming* play a key role here. Beliefs can have the power to appear to be real to us in the realm of thinking and feeling. This means we are usually not able to differentiate between what is real and what is only a belief. This is so powerful that it does not only affect our self-image and actions, but also how we perceive and feel about others and the entire world. All of us experience this when, for example, seeing the world through rose-colored glasses when being in love. In such a case, almost everything and everybody suddenly appears to be much more beautiful and nicer than usual. Whenever we change our view about others and the world, it is not the world or others that necessarily change, but our beliefs and feelings about them. This first part reflects how we perceive reality when we do not question what we are told and when we listen more to second-hand information than to our intuition. When I used to live according to this limiting perspective, my life was exhausting, also because I lived for others and not for myself. It was a life full of worries always living in the past and the future, rarely experiencing moments of deep peace and happiness. From this perspective, it seemed as if it were impossible to ever be fully free.

In the second part of each chapter, we bust those respective myths by pointing at *what may actually be happening*. It is essential to understand that this part does not intent to demonstrate the one and only right way of living, but instead does the following: firstly, it provokes our current beliefs and conditioning, which helps us to become aware of and eventually free from them. And secondly, it invites us to be open-minded towards a practical way of living that I and many other people since the beginning of mankind have found to work on many different levels.

The crucial point here is not to blindly adopt any preconceived wisdom or way of living, but to discover it afresh for ourselves; otherwise, our new way of living would be based, yet again, on another acquired belief. We are not interested in propaganda for a new movement, but in freeing ourselves from any movement, method or belief. Furthermore, we do not propose how one should or should not live one's life or what one should think about the world. It is not about learning *what* to think, but rather about *how* to think. As a natural consequence, we are able to live a more light-hearted and joyful life characterized by a peace of mind and authenticity without having to sacrifice our lifestyle.

While reading this book, it may help to direct your attention not so much on the words themselves, but more on the *perfume of the book*, from which the words spring and point towards. At the same time, I invite you to closely observe your reactions, judgments, thoughts and emotions triggered by what you are reading. This may help you to strengthen your intuition, one of the most valuable vehicles most of us have forgotten to use on our way to adulthood. You may also notice an inner dialogue or argument between what your thoughts tell you on the one hand and what messages your *heart* gives you on the other hand. I invite you to observe from moment to moment whether you give more credibility to thoughts or to your intuition. Whenever you observe yourself resisting or denying something expressed in this book – and also in life – put some extra attention on it as it may point to some hidden aspects looking for your attention.

This book is designed to be read either from the beginning to the end or for you to directly jump to specific chapters that you resonate with at the time you pick up the book. The sum of reading all chapters provides you with additional value painting a more holistic picture. Since this book is not about acquiring knowledge, but works on a more substantial level, you may also find some intentional repetitions that take effect on you, which by the way, works no matter how much you may agree or disagree with its content. Since life itself is a paradox, you may also encounter statements that may superficially seem to be inconsistent with other statements in the book. I invite you not to treat this book the same way you would treat a scientific paper because life itself does not follow scientific rules. It is rather the case that science tries to understand and simulate life.

Since this book is intended to be of highly practical nature, it includes guiding questions and space for notes after each chapter. If you like, you can use it as a practical workbook that could almost act as if it were your personal coach. It is for all people who want to roll up their sleeves and look for long-lasting remedy. When using it in that manner, and not in a purely theoretical way, you may be able to transform your life in a way you would have never been able to imagine. It can help to make your private life lighter and your relationships more fulfilling. At the same time, it can help to make your business more successful and increase your performance as an athlete. Discover what it means to be fully alive in your own life.

Keep in mind that the most essential element is not the book itself, but what meaning you give to it. Similar to quantum physics, in which the observer has the biggest influence on any experiment, you are by far the biggest influence on this book, not the author or its words. This book is nothing without you and can be everything with you. You are reading it based on all your conditioning, beliefs, memories, and perspectives about the world and yourself. Yet, the more you are able to seemingly let go of the latter, the more you will discover the dance of life that I experienced while I was writing it.

UPLIFTING AT ITS CORE

This is not a conventional book containing acquired knowledge as we may be used to. We do not read it to restock our knowledge base, hear about new theories or methods to then try if they work or not or discuss about them. It is not based on knowledge from the past, but it is designed to take us beyond the realm of thinking, that is, to a timeless *space,* whose nature is to make us feel fully alive.

At its core, this book is uplifting in its most radical, human form. While it uplifts our heart, it is provocative towards our limiting beliefs, which often times we identify with more than with our heart. The provocative statements are there to rattle our current image of the world. The intention is not to criticize any specific people or institutions or to create any conspiracy theories. The point is rather to challenge the status quo, which is far-off from any conspiracy. We usually do not see how our acquired knowledge from yesterday keeps us from seemingly being free at the given moment. Therefore, the provocative elements are also used to *slap or tickle* us out of the known allowing us to get a taste of our true nature. The choice is on our side: either we get caught up in the content defending our current point of view and judging this book to be provocative, or we stay open-minded enough to be able to challenge our own status quo.

At the end of the day, this book is not about itself, but about you! You do not care about this book, but about how to be able to live a life full of joy. Therefore, it is one thing to have insights while reading the book, and yet another to be able to translate those insights into actual life situations. We all have met people who have deep insights, but who do not apply them in most part of their lives. So, do not keep your insights in your head or show them off in conversations with your friends, but embody them in every given situation, whether you are by yourself or with others. Our journey on this pathless path is not about aiming to receive approval from society or others about our degree of wisdom, but about embodying wisdom in every step and breath we take.

OVERTURE – MY STARTING POINT IS FABRICATED

None are more hopelessly enslaved than those
who falsely believe they are free.
– Johann Wolfgang von Goethe, born in 1749

We are not who we think we are. We can read this statement in at least two different ways: firstly, we are more than our thinking and what we imagine to be, which means our essence is beyond what we are able to grasp with our mind. And secondly, we identify ourselves with something we are not. Both meanings play a role in this book. As a result of this misidentification, our days are characterized by an almost constant struggle. While we usually assume there is something wrong with the world, the system or other people, it rather seems as if there were something wrong with the way we approach life in every situation, that is, our starting point. Those of us, who claim to be fine despite the struggle, may not be aware of our true nature, having forgotten what it means to be fully alive. Throughout this book, I invite you to challenge the status quo of our world, and even more importantly, of our starting point, from which we approach every situation in life.

To illustrate what impact a wrong starting point can have on our life, let's take a look at a simple analogy. Imagine a big tray full of glasses, plates and silverware. The tray's surface is slippery and has just been tilted. As a consequence, all objects on the tray have slid down and some of them have fallen on the floor and broke. The people responsible for the tray try to solve the given challenge by setting up a non-slippery surface in between the spaces that they can reach on the tray, building protective cushions in between the glasses and plates to avoid scratches, setting up sophisticated noise cancellation devices and many other fancy high-tech solutions. To ensure the highest quality possible, they only hire highly recognized people who have a proven track record and know everything about the ideal materials to be used and about the given environmental factors, such as the impact of humidity on the glasses. Very quickly, the tray looks highly sophisticated and is equipped with state-of-the-art computer and engineering technology. They even set up call centers to keep the owners and investors of the glasses and silverware informed about the progress. Over time, more and more people get involved in this business. Once they manage to solve one particular issue, different issues appear in other areas of the tilted tray. While the implemented solutions never work for all objects, they mainly protect the glasses and silverware owned by the most influential people. Even without any bigger problems being present, people pretend to be busy managing one thing or another on the tray, although it may not make the overall situation better. Despite dealing with many problems, most people are very happy with the overall situation of the tray, are proud of their achievements and even make it their business to give each other rewards for outstanding achievements. Some of the best managers educate new generations of tray experts, who then apply the best practices from the generation before and even improve those further. The standard of the tray technology constantly improves. The people in the tray society are convinced they have the best tray in the world wondering whether there may be other trays on other planets.

If one day the *tray people* were approached by a humble, wise man telling them that the cause of all their problems lied in the tray being tilted, they would arrogantly laugh at him claiming he was crazy and not qualified for commenting on the tray. Since all of the *tray people's* jobs rely on the tray being tilted, nobody would even be open to entertain the possibility that the tilted tray is the core problem, even denying it to themselves, let alone daring to talk about it in public without being afraid of being judged by others. Another reason for not being open to identify the core problem is that all generations before had lived on the tray and all the important people in society support and lobby for the conventional tray business. Even if some of them had a clue about something being wrong with it, they had no choice but to play along the important *tray game* because it would be the only way to find acceptance and make it in this society.

In this analogy, the tilted tray represents our wrong starting point, on which we have seemingly built our entire reality. When starting from that wrong point, the world will always feel distorted, no matter how sophisticated our solutions may be, for the simple reason that we ignore what is actually happening. It is enough to clearly see that the tray is tilted, which reveals its true functioning nature, that is, being in balance. Seeing this may require being able to unlearn what we were indoctrinated with, being utterly honest with ourselves and standing up for the truth even if everyone else told us and acted as if the opposite were true.

1

You already are
what you are looking for

MYTH 1 – IT IS MORE IMPORTANT TO BE HAPPY LATER THAN NOW

He who is not contented with what he has, would not be contented with what he would like to have.
– Socrates, born in 470 BC

What we believe or seemingly experience to be true

We usually give more attention to the future than to how we feel at the present moment. Even while reading this sentence, we may be half *here* and half attached to our thought process planning the future. We think and say things such as I *will* be okay, hoping the future will be better than what life is currently presenting to us. Or put differently: we believe we can be happy once certain conditions are met, such as having enough money, the right partner, the right friends, the right job, good health or enough time.

An example of how we sacrifice our wellbeing in order to eventually benefit from something in the future is going to office every day where we spend time with people we do not connect with and do things we do not really like. We agonize over this because we believe that this is just the way life is, hoping in secret that one day we are able to do what we really like.

What may actually be happening

The very act of postponing our happiness gets in the way of being happy at the given moment. By making this a habit, we put ourselves in a constant chase for happiness forgetting what it means to feel fully alive. We ignore that life never takes place outside of the *now*, neither in the past nor in the future. We can never actually live in the future, but only *think* about it, the latter also taking place in the *now*. The future never becomes reality because by the time it *arrives*, it is again the present moment. This means, we spend most our time on something that does not even exist. By constantly planning to be happy in the future, we try to conserve and reproduce certain activities and moments that we think caused our happiness in the past and hope it will bring back the same feeling, without being aware that the very act of doing so causes us to suffer.

Something seems to be fundamentally wrong with our quest for happiness. It is as if we put the horses not before but behind the horse-drawn buggy. In this analogy, we try very hard to move the carriage forward – always with our best intentions. But every day, the result looks the same. The horses stumble right into the carriage pushing it a few yards forward, get hurt, dust themselves off and try again. Though certain experts, who provide us with professional advice on how exactly the horses should run, help us to make the process a bit smoother, they also oversee that the horses belong in front of the carriage. And although our intuition tells us something is wrong, we still continue to follow such a failed approach because everyone else does as well.

During waking hours, our attention is almost constantly on thoughts. Rare and short breaks only occur when we find relief by engaging in activities such as working out, taking drugs, engaging in spirituality, helping others, experiencing pain, meditating or eating, which are almost all exercises that make us listen more to our body. Our obsession with listening to the thought process is so strong that it almost seems as if we were *hypnotized* by or even *enslaved* to it. The nature of thoughts is to be either in the future or in the past. Thoughts are incapable of capturing the moment, in which everything is happening, including the thought process itself. The more our attention is directed to the thought process, the more nervous and anxious we become. And the more we put our attention away from thoughts, for instance, on observing an animal, our breathing, the sound of silence or the ocean, the more we are relaxed. This is true for every human being including celebrities, spiritual leaders, politicians, psychologists and athletes. Just as illustrated in the horse-drawn buggy analogy, the pattern of being glued to thoughts has been going on for many generations. Although it has not brought any permanent relief, we still look for our ultimate happiness by the same means that have failed us again and again. Why would we still hold on to something that does not serve us? The societal factor, which we do not challenge, plays a significant role in this. Society values how big our bank account and reputation is, but not how happy we are at a given moment, which immensely impacts our everyday behavior.

Most of us are not even aware that we are different from the thought process, mainly because we are fully identified with it. Although this idea as such seems to be absurd to many of us, paradoxically, it is the only way to be aware of our thoughts in the first place. If your tongue were made of salt and I put salt on your tongue, would you be able to taste it? Of course, you would not be able to do so – just as it is impossible for water to get wet. What perceives cannot be perceived. The same is true for thoughts. If we were made of thoughts, we would not be able to be aware of them. Being different from thoughts means we are free from them by nature.

The cause for putting our attention so obsessively on the thought process is the belief that thoughts are from and about us, which makes us interested in them in the first place. In the pursuit of finding remedy, calming our thoughts is one thing, recognizing they are not ours another. In the analogy from above, calming our thoughts would be equal to changing the speed and angle of how the horses run into the carriage. And understanding that thoughts are not about us would be to see that the horses belong in front of the carriage, which naturally puts our attention away from them. Discover more about our relationship with thoughts under *Myth 9* in this book.

Let's take a look at another aspect that makes us believe we are in a race for happiness. We would only be interested in becoming happy, if we were convinced that what we already are is different from happiness. It is very rare that we actually question this. Before jumping right into solving a problem, it is always wise to first challenge its underlying assumptions. Overlooking those often opens up the possibility for us to be a *victim* of manipulation. For instance, the advertising industry uses this strategy when artificially creating needs or wants. Smart marketing managers create a seeming need or want based on false, yet exciting assumptions telling a story that makes it appear to be true to us. Since the story sounds so promising, we silently agree to its logic overlooking its assumptions, and as a consequence, feel the urge to buy the product.

Furthermore, we are told happiness is something we can attain when pursuing certain goals or activities such as going to the right parties, having the right friends, having that amazing job, having that beautiful house and having much money. However, once we actually attain those things, we come to realize that what we were promised would not come – which is only obvious when understanding the mechanism behind happiness, which works as follows: contrary to our usual assumption that the cause of happiness is to be found in the object we desire, such as buying a house, getting that long-desired job or a new girlfriend, happiness is actually caused by the very act of letting go of that desire, which occurs right after we managed to achieve a certain goal. But instead of realizing that our moment of happiness is caused by that very act of letting go, we make the object itself responsible for having caused our moment of happiness. This puts us in a race for continuously chasing certain materialistic objects hoping the next one will make us ultimately happy. Although we know we eventually get bored with any object or person, even with the noblest man or most attractive woman in the world, we still do not make the connection. This also explains why we do not remain happy as long as we have the object of desire, such as that boyfriend or house, but are only happy as long as the relaxation remains. Chasing our desires on this realm is what is keeping us from being happy in the moment. See it for yourself in your own life. It is very obvious once we are no longer caught in this mechanism. Happiness is not derived from continuously running behind and reaching new goals, but is our very nature. Similarly, many of us try to become happy through practicing spirituality, finding our passion or reading self-help books, pretending to be better than the ones still chasing materialistic goals, without being aware that even spiritual seeking is part of trying to be happy in the future.

In my childhood, I never engaged in activities in order to become happy later; nor did I care whether I was naked in public, nor did I pretend I could be doing anything other than what I was doing at the given moment. I was fine with whatever happened, whether *good* or *bad.* Deep down, there was always this sense of joy and peace, which did not depend on any activities. I enjoyed observing my parents and other adults, but never understood why they were pretending to be so important when being around certain people. It seemed to be a very strange concept to me. I just thought to myself *This is adult business and I never want to be like them*. But at the same time, it made me very curious because they seemed to take their quest for happiness so seriously and pretended to know what they are doing. Eventually, I started to join that game, and every year, I implemented more and more elements of it. As a result, I got to experience moments of great excitement and pride, but on the flipside also moments of great isolation and sadness for the very first time. The more I went into this, the more exciting it became. For instance, I was looking for happiness in getting approval from others and in winning tennis matches. Since I got a kick out of that, I extended it to receiving good grades in school. I quickly came to understand that the higher something was valued by society, the more was at stake and the more exciting it was. I was attracted by statements and buzzwords such as *great party, how to become a successful tennis player, how to become rich* and *how to get a beautiful girlfriend.* The more serious I took this game, the more that sense of peace faded and the activities themselves, such as tennis, were no longer just fun. I thought to myself that once I am a great tennis player, have a beautiful girlfriend and have a job as a manager, I would be happy. Yet, once I reached all of the above, I was still not happy and felt I was lied to. I was wondering what all the people around me were doing. But when realizing that everyone around me was either still on the search for the next big thing or already gave in, I truly questioned the entire chase. The mere act of questioning my assumptions enabled me again to truly enjoy the game of tennis without trying to get something out of it. I realized that while the fitted happiness society tries to sell us depends on the approval of others, our true happiness does not depend on anything or anyone.

Similar to the way we chase happiness, we also try to get more into the moment. As long as we believe it were possible to get into the moment, we also believe it were possible to be ever out of the moment. However, our experience tells us that we can never *not* be in the *now.* Those of us who engage in mindfulness or mediation exercises to get more into the moment, sometimes say things such as *I had it, but I lost it again.* Trying to get into the moment is as if we tried to catch the moment by the means of thoughts, which is not possible by nature. What effort is involved in becoming what we already are? Will we achieve this by following certain methods? Or is it enough to see what we are not?

Happiness and the *now* are not goals we can attain but they are what we are made of. Seeking happiness outside ourselves would be the same as looking for our glasses while wearing them or as having the wish to go to California when we are already there. It just does not make any sense. It is not a coincidence that we hear people say that there is one common *goal* all of us share, which is to be happy. This is just another way of saying that we all want to come back *home* to happiness, which we have never left in the first place.

Now, before jumping into the question of *how* you can be happy, clearly see the mechanism behind happiness in the very moment life is happening. Become aware of the moments, in which you postpone your happiness, by for example hoping to be happy once you have a better job, a better partner, a better house or approval from others. How does this make you feel? And above all, entertain the possibility that you are already happiness itself and that every move towards it actually brings you further away. Find it out, not on an intellectual level comparing it with what you already know, but by closely observing your own experience right at this moment. Nobody else can do this for you.

Which activities do you do out of pure pleasure? And how much attention do you pay to their outcome?

....

....

....

....

....

Which activities do you primarily engage in to benefit from in the future? How do you feel while doing them?

....

....

....

....

....

SPACE FOR INSPIRATION & CREATIVITY

MYTH 2 – I CANNOT FOLLOW MY DREAMS BECAUSE I HAVE TO EARN MY LIVING

Respond to every call that excites your spirit.
– Rumi, born in 1207

What we believe or seemingly experience to be true

In the beginning and during the peak time of our career, we are eager to prove to the world that we are a good and worthy citizen. But once we successfully demonstrated our abilities, many of us no longer feel the pressure or need to make a mark within the conventional working environment. Instead, we feel it would be wiser to primarily follow our own dreams, and not to please or serve others to follow theirs.

Yet, during this decision-making process, many of us strongly hesitate to leave our secure job to do what really resonates with us, despite receiving clear signs from our intuition. Staying in our job seems to be the easier path, also because it is highly valued by society and even by our own reasoning. But at the same time, it means we have to continue to do something we do not enjoy. Being surrounded by people who themselves choose security over passion does not help either because we do not necessarily want to stand out from the crowd. Additionally, time is also not on our side; the longer we postpone following our dreams, the less likely we will ever pursue them.

For others that moment of truth might show up much earlier, much later or never in life, mainly depending on whether we listen more to our intuition or to society.

What may actually be happening

If we think life is all about conforming to society, the best thing to do is to hold on to our seemingly secure job, even though we may not truly enjoy it. But if we think life is primarily about being fully alive in its truest and freest form, it is wise to follow our heart.

When we are not sure whether to leave our job, the following question may help us to find the answer: would we continue staying in our current job if we did not get paid? If the answer is *no*, we most likely live a life based on a socially accepted compromise. One typical symptom of this lifestyle is that we feel the happiest on weekends and during a vacation and have a hard time going to office on Mondays. In case we believe we are fully alive despite the described symptoms, it may be useful for us to dive into the question of what *feeling fully alive* actually means. If the answer is *yes*, we may either not be honest with ourselves or already do what comes naturally to us.

Holding on to a conventional job is a false security. We can never find security outside of us – neither in a job, nor in relationships, nor in any other seesawing life circumstances, no matter how strongly we hold on to something. We are given the impression by our parents, teachers and friends that having a job gives us ultimate security. But have you ever challenged this assumption? What does it secure: our freedom or rather our obedience? Does it help us to think freely or rather reinforce our conformation to society? We assume that having a conventional job is a given in life in the same way as it is a given for the body to breathe. We never truly question this although the majority of people suffer on so many different levels related to going to work every day. The reason for engaging in something we do not enjoy in the first place, and doing so every day for most days of our life, is that everybody else is doing the same. We do not dare to behave differently from the mass because we are afraid of being judged and not being accepted by others.

Ask yourself the following: would you still be in your job if you were the only one working in the conventional sense; if everyone else were free to do whatever they truly enjoy? I am sure you would tell your boss where to get off for keeping you like a *slave*. We have come to believe that our society can only function properly if most of us have a *proper job*, that is, sacrificing to be fully alive serving others as a productive machine for them to achieve their often greedy goals. Paradoxically, we do not even perceive ourselves as *slaves,* but instead as very important people, also thanks to having a great reward system in place. We have seemingly been *brainwashed* to such a degree that we even feel empty and unworthy when not having a job. Just to be clear, we are obviously not saying in any way that it is bad to be active in life. We are actually saying the opposite: we can only be truly active when we are free and fully alive. It is usually too much for our reasoning to understand that we can be free *and* have a high standard of living at the same time. The incapability of understanding this just shows the high degree of conditioning we go through.

Since following our dreams is also closely related to the idea of having to earn a living, let's take a small excursion into the world of money. Have you ever taken a moment to understand what money really is? We do not mean the mere technical part of how it creates scarcity and how the interest-debt system works, but we are referring to what money is in its most practical form. When fundamentally looking at this, it becomes clear that it is not money that has the inherent ability to build or create something, but it is always people. Now, imagine we abolished money right in this moment, and hence, it no longer existed in this world – which, by the way, was the case for most of human history. What major changes would we observe? Would plants still grow food? Would people still be able to construct buildings? Would you still stay in your job? In theory, the world could go on as it is keeping the same standard of living because no money in the world has ever grown fruits, built houses or healed humans. And even machines, products and raw materials are not produced by money, but by people. However, in practice, the world would significantly change because we would lose a major instrument to manipulate people. Additionally, we would most likely observe a shift in power over resources and property and people getting out of their jobs.

Obviously, we do not suggest abolishing money here, but it is noteworthy to point out that there is not only one way of earning money, but there are as many ways as there are people. To earn money, it is enough that there are people who perceive some kind of value in what we do, no matter what it is – even if nobody has ever made money that way before. While money plays an important role in the decision-making process, the main motivation for staying in our job is rather the highly conditioned state-of-mind described earlier in this chapter, especially the fear of not being accepted by others.

The point of this chapter is not to make you quit your job, but to raise awareness of the mechanisms behind you staying in a conventional job. In your specific case, it may be the right thing to quit your job right away, in five years or never – only life itself has the answer to this. To give an example of such a journey, I quit my conventional job after having gone through an inner process that had lasted for several years. Through the obtained clarity at the end of the inner journey, it was the most natural thing for me to quit. At the end, I realized that it did not serve me to have a life, in which I seemingly mute my intuition and the very source of life. The more I tried to do that, the more numb I felt inside and the more of a compromise my entire life became, although to the outside, my life seemed to be brilliant. We usually numb ourselves to such a degree that we even forget what it means to be fully alive in the first place, many times without being aware of what exactly is going on. I also learned that those who hardly ever listen to their heart might falsely believe to be stronger than others without being aware that they are just *better* at obeying and conforming to authorities, thanks to their strong stamina. Being successful within society does not necessarily make us freer or bring us closer to truth.

Life is very simple. It is enough to follow our intuition and the signs life gives us at any given moment. We do not necessarily have to analyze the past and take big decisions for the future, but can decide from moment to moment. Furthermore, we do not have to desperately try to find our passion to then follow it. Life is not a conceptual or single-minded process. It is rather momentary and paradoxical. Whenever we encounter resistance, it shows us that we are unnecessarily holding on to something. Whenever things come to us naturally or we are able to do them with ease, it shows that we are going with the flow of life. At any given moment, we choose either freedom or fear. The more we choose fear, the more we suffer. The more we choose freedom, the more we are ready to do what we truly enjoy. The more aware we are of the bigger picture, the more it is not us who choose freedom, but it is freedom or grace choosing us. In other words, we stop playing God and let the *omni-intelligent* life force take over. In this process, it may happen that instead of working as a businesswoman or lawyer – which we primarily do to prove something to us or others – we may be doing what we intrinsically enjoy, such as writing a book, painting, singing or healing others. At the end of the day, it is more beneficial to have a short life that is full of what we enjoy than a long life that we spend in a compromised way.

Would you continue to stay in your job even if you did not receive any money? Why or why not?

If money were no object, how would you spend your time? What activities would you engage in?

SPACE FOR INSPIRATION & CREATIVITY

MYTH 3 – I NEED TO PUSH AWAY MY FEAR

These pains you feel are messengers. Listen to them.
– Rumi, born in 1207

What we believe or seemingly experience to be true

We want more of what makes us feel good and push away what makes us feel uncomfortable assuming the latter is enough to clear the way.

When encountering fear, we apply the same principle. Fear makes us feel very unpleasant, and hence, we try to avoid it, which we do mainly for two reasons: firstly, we hope we do not have to go through the pain of experiencing unpleasant feelings, and secondly, we hope we can hide it from others. We usually do not express fear, vulnerability or weakness in public because we feel guilty for being afraid thinking something may be wrong with us or it could hurt our reputation. Instead, we rather build walls around us muting our feelings, both good and bad, which, in turn, makes us feel numb and empty as opposed to fully alive.

While we hope that not confronting or ignoring fear will be enough for it not to come back, we know from experience that by doing so it rather stays with us, grows bigger or may find expression in form of an illness or an accident. Since unfinished fears usually show up in quiet moments, we try to avoid those as much as possible by keeping ourselves busy through work, family, entertainment or friends. By the way, this avoidance is also one of the reasons many of us have trouble sleeping.

What may actually be happening

The nature of feelings is to come and go like clouds in the sky. No matter how dark or thick the clouds are, they never leave any traces in the sky. In a similar way, feelings never touch us in our essence, although sometimes it may appear to us they do.

There are two common approaches when dealing with *negative* emotions. On the one hand, when allowing any feeling to come to us unconditionally, we are able to fully embrace and confront it without any resistance; and naturally, it leaves again. On the other hand, when interfering with a feeling in one way or the other, for example by pushing it away, we store it in our body. As a consequence, it visits us again and again, usually in situations, in which we show most resistance. A good sign for noticing we resist is when we deny a certain habit or feeling. This denial almost always means we actually do what we deny, but do not want to admit it to others and not even to ourselves. For instance, when my wife approached me saying I was impatient in a certain situation, I told her right away, out of reaction, that this was not true. However, the fast denial and reaction is a very good sign that I was actually impatient. The denial also did not allow me to look further into what my wife told me, but pushed it away, so the situation continued to stay with us and popped up again at a later stage.

Without any reason, we usually consider feelings such as fear as something *negative*, just like weed in a garden. When experiencing negative feelings, we think something might be wrong with us or we failed because we picture a successful life to be free of them altogether. But life is not a competition, in which the one with the fewest negative feelings wins. Feelings are not there to make our life harder, but serve the purpose of showing us whether we are on the right track or whether someone or something needs attention. For instance, a negative feeling could tell us to pay more attention to our body, a friend is in trouble or someone sitting next to us in a train is going through a hard time.

By identifying with feelings, we are obsessed with them and become prone to the possibility of getting hurt in the first place. Since by doing so we assume they are about us, we are so busy pushing them away to not get hurt that we are not even able to listen to their message. We are only ready to fully confront a feeling when being aware we are not the feeling itself, but the one noticing it. At the same time, for most of us, this seems as if it were an impossible act because most of our identification is with thoughts and feelings. Hence, it would appear to us as if we had to give away some part of who we are.

Life usually communicates with us in a very light and gentle manner, which can easily be missed, especially when paying more attention to the much *louder* thoughts and feelings. The more we ignore its subtle messages, the stronger they become. At some point, they may even become so strong that it feels as if life *slapped us in the face*, which, for instance, could happen in form of getting chronically sick, having an accident, getting injured, a death of a close one or something else. I had been to hospital for one smaller and one major accident. In both instances, at the time they occurred, I perceived them as some of the worst things that ever happened to me. But looking back, I thought they were some of the best things because I received profound life lessons. During the years before the particular accidents, I had been trying to ignore and push away my fears and had become very inventive in doing so. Being mentally strong made me believe I could live that way forever. But by forcingly trying to live without ever experiencing any fear, I was no longer in touch with my feelings – which I was not even aware of. I was stuck in a dead end and life could no longer reach me in a soft manner because my mind had become too strong and resistant. Therefore, I needed a major *slap* in form of a few surgeries and a seven-week hospital stay to bring me back in touch with life.

Taking a closer look at fear, we are never afraid of a certain object or idea, but of fear itself; although, we may claim we are afraid of spiders, snakes, small rooms, height, failure and so on. For instance, when saying we are afraid of snakes, the snake is neither the problem nor the cause of the fear, but *only* its trigger. Understanding this is the first step in letting go of fear. The true remedy is not to make a person like snakes again, but to get right at the cause of the fear. Of course, through certain methods, it would be possible to get someone used to snakes again without an outbreak of fear, but unless the cause of the fear is taken care of, it would come up in form of fear of heights or spiders, for example. Yet, most of our so-called experts in society are trained to treat symptoms and not to remove causes. While it is relatively easy to learn to follow certain methods to treat symptoms, it is almost impossible to teach someone getting at the cause, which requires an utmost presence and clarity.

This also gives us a hint that we can only transfer knowledge, but not wisdom. While shallow knowledge may help us to earn much money and be recognized in society, it does not help us to get rid of fear – because the latter requires wisdom that we can only experience first-hand.

Generally, we can say there are two different kinds of fear. There is the spontaneous, biological fear that comes and goes with situations, such as facing a wild animal or hanging on a cliff. This probably accounts for much less than one percent of fear. The other kind of fear is of psychological nature and seemingly disturbs our peace of mind every day. It is an imaginary fear, that is, a fear of something that only exists within our imagination. Being afraid of something that does not exist is *normally* called *insanity*. At the same time, it is socially accepted because most of us suffer from it on a daily basis. But instead of getting right at its cause and finding a long-lasting solution for all, we try to build our life around fear; also because there are still too many people benefiting from people with fear on many different levels. We are only able to experience this kind of fear if we are seemingly identified as a body-mind, believing we are separate from life and other people. The body-mind construct does not have a separate reality in its own, but we constantly lend it our reality, *it* always being afraid of being caught. Clearly seeing this mechanism would mean the body-mind loses its identity, and as a consequence, we would live a life free of fear. To illustrate this, let's take a look at a snake that is in the process of changing its skin. From the perspective of the snake, there is nothing better than getting a new, moisturized and smooth skin. But from the perspective of the current skin, it is the worst thing that could ever happen because it fears its own death. For every move the snake makes, the skin is horrified and afraid, especially when going over some *tricky* rocks or when staying in the sun for too long. The same is true for us. The body-mind construct is afraid of being caught for the illusion it represents, and as a consequence, we fight against the natural flow of life every day, not being aware what we truly are is freedom.

Primarily, we have been concerned with discovering a *condition*, in which fear can no longer be a problem. Since it may also be practical to get temporary relief from an existing fear, we will briefly cover one example showing what we can do when facing a reoccurring, negative emotion. A few years ago, I heard about a therapist who very effectively works with her clients not in the usual, isolated office environment, but in the very surrounding, in which a certain fear is triggered. In a specific case, she asked her client who suffered from a fear of heights to climb up a high ladder. The client was occupied with fear before he stepped on the ladder, it intensified when he was making his way up and peaked right on top. As soon as she told him to climb down again, the fear significantly decreased. And when he was still on the ladder on his way down and was asked whether he was still afraid, he noticed he was not, foreseeing that he would be on the ground again in the next moment. Feeling that he could be on the ladder without being afraid helped him to get rid of the fear in that session because he realized the fear was not caused by the height, but by an idea and resistance in his body-mind. Understanding this on the level of the body and not just intellectually was key. It was one of those moments when it *clicked* for him. What usually also helps is to remind us on a feeling level that there was once a time when we were not afraid of heights, that is, demonstrating that the fear started at a certain point of time. That way we are able to experience that fear is not something given or inherent, but something that comes after our own essence, and hence, is separate from us.

In some instances, we think we can get around fear by hiding it to others and even ourselves. While it may work that nobody else notices the fear, we can never lie to life or our body. Our body remembers everything. Hiding fear also reflects what we value in society, that is, it is more important what others think of us than how we actually feel. Once we realize we do not live for or *report to* others, we feel no longer forced to try to hide anything because we come to understand that thoughts and feelings are not private. Not others, but life itself is our ultimate authority, which does not have any of the fearful attributes human authorities may have. Understanding this helps us to become more authentic in everything we do.

When dealing with *negative* feelings, the following point is also essential to understand. There is a fine, but significant difference between unconditionally allowing *negative* feelings to show up to confront them and getting lost in a spiral of negativity. The latter is something most of us engage in every day. However, we are not to follow negativity, but to confront it with openness being aware we are not the feeling itself. This awareness allows us to appropriately deal with fear and process feelings the moment they occur.

Above all, no matter how attached we may be to feelings, or how dark and thick the clouds are, the sky, that is, what we are, is never affected in the slightest way. Being aware of this provides us with a different kind of quality when dealing with emotions. Even if conventional therapists try to convince us of the opposite, knowing we can never be affected by any traumas or feelings means we are able to live in true freedom.

What are your greatest fears? How do they show up and how do you deal with them?

At the very moment you are afraid, in which part of the body do you notice something uncomfortable? What exactly do you feel?

SPACE FOR INSPIRATION & CREATIVITY

2

You are invincible

MYTH 4 – JUDGING MAKES ME STRONGER

If God listened to the prayers of men, all men would quickly have perished: for they are forever praying for evil against one another.
Epicurus, born in 341 BC

What we believe or seemingly experience to be true

Judging has become second nature to us. We judge others, the world and ourselves every day, very often even without being aware of it. Somehow, it seems we can relieve stress by putting others down or labeling them. Furthermore, we think judging is necessary to form opinions, be assertive and protect our rights. In other words, we practice it to keep our chin up. But at the same time, the very act of judging makes us feel tense and isolated rather than relaxed and content.

When being judged by another, we often judge him in return. This helps us to discredit him, and hence, protect our worthiness or our feeling of being good enough towards others and ourselves. The more popular and credible the person judging is, the more painful it is because our reputation may not only be damaged in front of him, but potentially also in front of many others.

We grow up noticing how our parents judge neighbors, friends, colleagues, politicians, and celebrities, getting the impression that everyone is bad except for our parents. Without being aware most of the times, we automatically take on the judgments of our parents and look at the world accordingly. Furthermore, we get the impression that people who strongly judge others are important and powerful, because according to how bad they talk about everyone else, they seem to do everything right. Yet, when it comes to us, we feel that it is not right to judge, but still do it and even judge us for judging, which puts us in a vicious circle.

What may actually be happening

When we judge, it does at least two things to us: firstly, it demonstrates a lack and a seeming weakness, and secondly, it puts us into a low-spirited mood or energy. The main reason we compare and judge in the first place is that we hold on to the assumption of being separate from everything else. Only due to this false starting point, we feel this inner lack and insecurity, and as a consequence, we believe we have to fight for our rights, put others down to feel stronger than them, plan the future, become a respected citizen and protect us, so others do not take everything away from us. Even hearing about inspirational quotes from successful people saying we shall not compare and judge does not really refrain us from doing so because our wrong starting point requires us to continue to judge. A safe way to stop judging in the long run is not to treat the symptoms, but to go after the root cause, which is seeing that we are not a separate, long-lasting independent entity.

At the moment of judging, we reside in a low-spirited state, which is usually preceded by feelings of anger, hate or fear. The more we feel unhappy, the more we judge. And the more we judge, the more it puts us down even more. While judging may help us to temporarily relieve stress, it makes us suffer the moment after. In contrast, when we are truly happy, there is no motivation to judge or put others down. Think of the people in your life who are most judgmental about others or themselves. Do they behave that way out of a state of happiness or rather out of insecurity or hate?

We never compare apples with apples when judging. In a way, judging is as if we took a water sample from a river, putting it in a cup and pretending to know the river by solely referring to the water sample and not the river itself. We all know the river is so much more than just a water sample. The same is true when judging others. For instance, if we judge someone to be nice for holding the door open for us in a restaurant, it does not mean he would not be able to harm someone, although the judgment excludes that. Similarly, a so-called *criminal* may be overall more considerate and compassionate than certain teachers, but labeling him a *criminal* would not do justice to who he is in life in general. The point here is that no label, thought or word will ever be able to describe the depth of any human being. We all have thousands of different *faces* that constantly change. Just because we dress in a certain way, engage in certain activities, come from a certain country or have a certain skin color does not mean we always act in a certain expected way based on a judgment. Life and each one of us is much larger than any label would ever be able to express. It will never be possible to catch who we truly are with a net made of thoughts.

Although we usually think it is the other way around, judgments say more about the one judging than the person being judged. For instance, when hearing about someone complaining about the bad service in a hotel, it is all about the expectations, associations and emotions of the person judging. In the same hotel, there are always people who are happy with the very same service, which can only be possible if the judgment is not about the object being judged, but about the one who judges. Else, every service would get the same review, independent of the one experiencing it. Or take a book as another example. Although every reader reads the exact same words, some of them may find it inspiring, while others may not resonate with it.

The more we judge others, the more we also judge ourselves, and vice versa. Just see it for yourself. I once had a manager who was very nice overall, but in many instances, very harsh. I always thought that she was just a strong woman who knows what she wants. But later I came to the clear understanding that she was very insecure with herself and projected this onto others by strongly judging and trying to put pressure on them. As a result, the entire team was constantly under unnecessary pressure.

We think judging is important because we act as if we had free will. For example, when hearing about a successful businessman, artist or millionaire, we try to understand his success model by analyzing and judging it, hoping we can reproduce his success in one way or another. Dependent on our expertise and background, some of us may see the key to success in his values, some others in his attitude, and again some others in the business strategies and methods he used. We all hope to be able to copy his success by following the magic key element as if his success were based on a model, just as an architect would use one to build a villa. But this is not the case. Life does not work that way. If it did, we would all become millionaires by applying *the famous ten steps* another millionaire had followed. The point is that becoming rich was not in the control of the millionaire, and hence, there is never a need to compare, judge or follow others.

All of us who perform at a high level, whether in athletics, business or life in general, know that comparing and judging hinder us from unlocking our full potential. During my time as a semi-professional tennis player, I remember experiencing a shift in performance by a few levels by clearly understanding the power of not judging. At the beginning, when I started to practice this, I felt a bit insecure because judging had previously been second nature to me; but after a certain time without judging, not only was my performance through the roof, but I also felt much more at ease and used less energy on the court. We can only become aware of it when we experience this first hand. Someone telling us about it and then arguing about whether he is right or wrong is not enough. It is also not enough if we assume we do not judge. I have met many people who claim they do not judge, but when spending some time with them in their routine, it becomes obvious that they strongly do. It used to be the same for me. So, if you notice some thoughts in your mind telling you that you are very special and never judge, then look again. This might be a good indication that you actually do.

Judging gives us a false sense of security. When we judge, we feel powerful, and when we try to let go of judging, we feel powerless and insecure as if we gave up and lost our position that we worked for so hard. We can best observe this effect when looking at sports. For instance, most tennis players I have seen and worked with on the court, have a very hard time to let go of judging. They strongly judge every single ball they hit. When they hit a ball well, they are happy and when they miss, they are angry, which is an immense *waste* of energy. On surface, they feel better when judging and playing bad than if they do not judge and play well. But this *feeling better* is that very false sense of security. The reason they judge in the first place is to fill their seeming lack inside, which hinders them from unleashing their full potential. Every single player who manages to let go of judging on the court plays a few levels better. But most players are too attached to let go over a longer period of time. Those who not just think they should not judge, but embody it are the ones who end up playing the best tennis. As explained above, it is almost impossible to let go of judging as long as we are identified with being a separate entity. But it is the easiest thing in the world when being aware that we are not separate from the flow of life. What is true for tennis also applies to business and life in general, although the effect is more immediate in sports.

Since judging others can reveal interesting aspects about us, it is worth taking a closer look at such instances. For example, if a woman envied another woman for being authentic, open-minded and confident in public speech, it could mean that the woman judging may restrict herself from doing the same, that is, she feels insecure and is not herself when speaking in public. This could be due to someone restricting her during her upbringing, from which she could not free herself, yet. Maybe someone told her to listen to and adapt to others, not stand out and have good manners. At some point, her restrictions became reality and ever since, she has been caught in a trap of her beliefs. And when she sees people expressing *her freedom*, she is reminded of her own desire to be free.

Having personal or cultural prejudices is also part of comparing and judging. The less we *know* about other people or cultures from first-hand experience, the more prejudices we usually have. Out of our own insecurity, we try to understand the world through comparing and judging. We judge neighbors, people from close-by villages, celebrities we only know from media, people from other countries, people with other skin colors, people following other religions, and so on. We judge them without having ever really met, tried to understand or listened to them. The more we listen to people from various backgrounds, the more we realize we have more in common with them than we assumed. Ultimately, we all have something in common that is closer to us than any thought. For instance, when I lived in the United States in my early twenties, I overcame most of my cultural prejudices by just being open-minded to how people from different countries achieve the same results using different manners. We usually grow up thinking that our way of doing things, whether as part of our family, circle of friends, country, religion or company, is the right one. But after having traveled to different countries and understanding other cultures, always in combination with having an open mind, we come to realize that the terms right and wrong lose their meaning. When judging or labeling, we do not truly interact with a human being, but merely with an image we have of them, which neither allows them nor us to meet in a space of beauty and innocence. True compassion and love takes place in our essence beyond the form, beyond what we will ever be able to label.

Another commonly practiced form of judging is gossiping, which has contributed to making judging socially acceptable, especially through the countless gossip magazines that are read by millions of people every day. The more we read gossip magazines, the worse we feel about the world and ourselves.

We seemingly entered the vicious circle of judging, being unaware that we were never actually separated from anything or anybody in the first place. The moment we realize this, all the comparing and judging will naturally drop without any effort on our side. While at first, we may feel as if we were in a free fall and had nothing to hold on to anymore, we gradually come to realize that a life without judgment means freedom, and allows the sense of false security to be replaced by ultimate security, which can never be grasped by any thought, judgment or comparison.

Become aware of the moments, in which you judge yourself and others. In what mood do you find yourself just before?

Observe when someone else judges you. Does he or she act out of compassion or fear? Elaborate on your answer.

SPACE FOR INSPIRATION & CREATIVITY

MYTH 5 – I NEED TO GET RID OF MY EGO

Stop acting so small.
You are the universe in ecstatic motion.
– Rumi, born in 1207

What we believe or seemingly experience to be true

We hear and read about the term *ego* quite frequently and assume all of us give it the same meaning. At the same time, when taking a closer look at the term, we encounter many contradicting statements. On the one hand, people say it is bad to have an ego or it is not good to be egocentric. On the other hand, they tell us the ego is something good to have and it is not about getting rid, but about having a healthy amount of it – not too much, but also not too little.

Now, which statements are right? Is it good or bad to have an ego? Do we all have one? And what is an ego in the first place? What does it mean when we say our ego gets hurt? Are we the ego or is it something separate from us? Even when asking experts about what it really is, we usually do not get a clear answer. Why is it that something so close to us and so closely related to our happiness, confidence and success is not clear?

What may actually be happening

Clearly understanding the term ego is essential because it keeps us immune to psychological deception and may even help us to save many years of unnecessary seeking. Assuming we already know what ego is can seemingly *endanger* our peace of mind. Without being clear about it, we depend on so-called experts to tell us what it is, which puts our journey of finding out more about ourselves in the hands of others and makes us jump from one method to the next. But once we embody this clarity, we no longer have to believe gurus, psychologists and other experts telling us about how to tame the ego in the right way or how complicated it may be to ever become happy.

The term ego has several different practical meanings, depending on the context and the people using it. Most commonly, it is referred to either as self, self-esteem, or self-centeredness. Since we usually say we *have* an ego, and not we *are* one, there may be evidence that we are not the ego, but separate from it. If we were to look for proof of the existence of the ego, we were neither able to pinpoint it somewhere in the body, nor inside the brain in form of a physical object, which may give us a hint that it is rather of conceptual nature.

When referring to the ego as a *self*, it can be understood as an illusionary reference point that is seemingly fabricated and maintained by thoughts and believed to be true by that which is real, that is us. We refer to the ego as a reference point because we believe everything in the world is not just happening, but is seemingly happening *to* someone, which we call our self or ego. However, the ego never had and never will have an existence in its own. As opposed to our assumption, it does not exist prior to any actions, perceptions, feelings or thoughts, but it is always produced post-rationally after each event, claiming it was the doer, in form of the body-mind or the ego. It can only appear to exist as an idea in the realm of thoughts and time, that is, only in the past and the future, but never in the *now*; that is why the now is one of the most *boring places* for the ego. What happened is that the illusionary reference point seemingly *hijacked* the body-mind by identifying with it and uses this as a seeming proof of having an existence in its own. For many of us this is hard to grasp in the realm of thoughts because our identification with the self or body is so strong that we do not see how we could exist outside of them. As always, do not believe what you are reading here. It is enough to look at this in your own life. For instance, when claiming you made a decision, look closely at whether it was really you or whether it occurred and you afterwards claimed to be the one making it. Today, there are several experiments from psychology and neuroscience showing that decisions are made seconds before the brain even becomes aware of them.

We call the ego illusionary because, as mentioned above, it does not have a reality in its own, separate from everything else. However, this does not mean that we do not feel as if it were real. It seemingly appears to be real for most of us. But since it is illusionary by nature, the point is that it is not only possible to be free from it, but that we have never been the ego in the first place, which is a fine, but significant difference setting us completely free; not sometime in the future, for example, after practicing self-improvement for 20 years, but in no time.

When clearly becoming aware that the ego is something different from us, we can be free *from* it, not *as* it. By definition, the ego can never be free because its seeming existence is limited to the realm of thoughts. Most of the times, though, when following all of those self-improvement and mindfulness trends, we try to become free *as* the ego, which still means we are not free *from* it. The reason we want to become free as the ego is that we believe we are it. Yet, this activity still takes place and keeps us within the hamster wheel. I had been running in this hamster wheel for many, many years. If you had asked me back then whether I was stuck, I would have said *no* because I did not even see I was in it. I always tried to become free *as* the body-mind, *as* the self and *as* the ego. While that way I may have managed to become calmer, be more accepting and gain a stronger presence, I was still restricted to the very limitations of the body, mind and the reference center I was taking myself to be. I was judging other seekers and spiritual people for not being calm or not having a soft enough voice because they did not fit into my image of what it means to be free. Looking back, I can see that I confused my true nature, the formless, with the nature of the body-mind, and hence, wanted to become free as the form, not knowing that I was already free. Paradoxically, in most of science and everything we deal with every day, this confusion is common practice. When identifying as a self, we would also identify with statements such as *It is important to have an ego* or *I have to get rid of it,* which are all irrelevant from the perspective of who we are.

Not only is there confusion about the term ego regarding *self*, but also regarding *self-esteem* and *self-centeredness*. What the different meanings have in common is that they refer to something illusionary.

When making statements such as *You hurt my ego*, we speak about the ego in terms of *self-esteem*. Being identified with the body-mind and making our self-esteem dependent on what others say or do to us, it appears to us as if it were us who get hurt when being offended, which is actually never the case. As a defense mechanism, we usually try to protect the ego or self-esteem by building walls or limiting our activities to only those that are safe. That way, we try to avoid situations or people as much as possible to not get hurt again, which restricts our life significantly. Instead, the true way out is to seemingly drop the identification altogether, becoming aware that we never were the self-esteem in the first place.

We usually call those people selfish who foremost care about themselves, not being aware that being identified with a body-mind represents *self-centeredness itself*, meaning we constantly act from a point of selfishness. At the same time, it is essential to see that neither we nor others are ever truly that self-centeredness. Paradoxically, the less we are attached to the belief of being an ego, the more compassionate we are with others, although it is never really possible to be attached to the ego in the first place.

We are afraid of letting go of our attachments and beliefs as a self because we think the whole system would collapse, being unaware that by holding on to this illusionary reference center, we actually prevent life from fully flowing through us. We put so much pressure on ourselves thinking we have to manage our life. But maybe, it is not necessary to play *God*, and it is enough to trust a power far more intelligent than what we take ourselves to be. When being aware that we are neither a reference point, nor self-esteem, nor self-centeredness, we may still encounter feelings of being isolated, pain or greed, but the significant difference versus before is that we no longer identify with the feelings we notice, which allows us to be free *from* and not free *as* the ego.

This chapter is not about giving us new ideas on who we are, but is an invitation to understand what we are not – not for the sake of philosophizing, but in order to live freely and go through life in a more lighthearted way. Knowledge from experts such as psychologists and therapists about the ego seems to be correct and useful for many, but always only from the perspective of the ego. The same is true for attending relaxation courses, practicing yoga or meditating. While such knowledge and practice may be useful to improve our life *as* a self, it will never be able to take us beyond it, or put differently, it won't help us to be fully alive. Participating in the discussion about the ego and trying to become free *as* it would be the same as running in the hamster wheel pretending we are not in it. The good thing is that we do not have to follow any of this knowledge, but it is enough to clearly see what we are not, including the ego in all of its different forms. The only way out is to realize the hamster wheel is not motorized, stop running and be free not *as* the ego, but *from* it, which allows us to embody our true nature. See this for yourself in your daily activities. As Paul Hedderman would say: *the fastest way to get out of something is to realize we were never in it.*

Write down everything you identify with (e.g. family, nationality, sex, body, thoughts, religion).

Who or what are you without any of the identifications from the answer above? What is it that remains?

SPACE FOR INSPIRATION & CREATIVITY

MYTH 6 – I HAVE TO DEFEND AND JUSTIFY MYSELF

You were born with wings,
why prefer to crawl through life?
– Rumi, born in 1207

What we believe or seemingly experience to be true

When people offend us, we feel the impulse to defend ourselves and tell them off. We get heavily emotionally involved and *throw back* counter-arguments at them. The more we resist and defend the image we have of ourselves, the more hurtful it is for us.

In society, we are obsessed with our reputation to such a degree that we use it as if it were a currency. It is more important what certificates, awards and titles we collect and what certain people think of us than whether we show compassion or implement true, sustainable impact. We usually spend more time and energy on managing our reputation and pleasing others than on focusing on the actual activities. Building and defending our reputation is the most exhausting *business* we do every day, which not only managers and employees can tell us a thing or two about. It is so tiring because it always requires someone to approve our performance, which is all that counts at the end of the day. We act as if someone trying to harm our reputation were worse than injuring our arm.

Protecting our reputation is so important to us because we base our self-esteem on it. The latter depends on aspects such as what goals we achieve, our grades in school, our choice of wardrobe, how high up we are on the career ladder, how beautiful and big our house is or how powerful the people are we hang out with.

What may actually be happening

At some point in our childhood, we started to join this reputation game and became more and more absorbed in it. While in the beginning it might have been a playful thing to do, over time it turned into a dead serious business, in which we are seemingly stuck as an adult. We never challenged it at its core, also because somehow, we think we have to play along and adjust if we want to make it in this society. Almost all of us practice this every day, for instance, when wearing a mask at work or when trying to impress someone. Once this practice turns into a life attitude, which it does for most of us, we are enslaved to this reputation business. In the following paragraphs, we shed light on the mechanisms that keep us stuck in defending and justifying ourselves. By becoming aware of those, we will be able to stop scattering our energy, and instead, start engaging in uplifting activities such as making a real impact while fully embodying who we are.

We pretend there is only one truth out there, which makes us divide everything into right and wrong. This includes the world as such, opinions, political parties, forecasts about future events, recalling past events and everything else. Dividing the world into right and wrong forces us to constantly defend the truth and also convince others of it, for instance, when speaking to a friend or colleague or when reading an article in the newspaper. When others agree with our image of the world, we categorize them as the ones we like and who also see the truth, and if they disagree with us, we assume they are ignorant and need to be educated by us or other wise ones. However, contrary to our belief, the concept of right and wrong is not something that is pre-defined and a given in the world out there, but is something each one of us brings into the world. We give everything all the meaning it has. Due to the latter, it is possible to have disagreements in the first place, and we need judges to tell us the seeming truth – although judges are never able to give us the truth, but only their opinions. It is not our job to convince others of *the* truth because there are as many truths as there are people. Next time you hear someone say the opposite of what you believe to be true about a certain topic or even about yourself, just observe the reflex of wanting to correct your counterpart. Instead of wondering whether it would work or not, be open to experience it and see how it makes you feel. As a result, life will become more relaxing and you can finally use your energy on what really matters.

In certain situations, we sense a need to defend ourselves because we assume offenses are about the receiver. But when looking at it more closely, we quickly come to realize that they do not have anything to do with the receiver, but with the one offending. Why is that? The offender always acts from a low-spirited condition such as lack, anger or hate. If this were not the case, they would not even try to offend us. See this for yourself the next time your friend or partner blames you for something. Instead of reacting, listen fully and observe the situation including your impulse of wanting to react. The thing you are blamed for is never the cause, but if at all, the trigger for someone's offense. For instance, let's assume your friend Lisa is jealous and disappointed with you because you went on a vacation with her best friend Anna. Lisa is afraid you may now be closer to Anna than her. You truthfully did not have any bad intentions and it did not occur to you that going on a vacation with Anna could hurt her. The cause of Lisa's affront is her insecurity and sense of possessiveness, but not you going on a vacation with Anna. Unless Lisa clarifies her insecurities, she will continue to affront the people around her blaming them to be the cause for her misery, even if they treat her with compassion.

As soon as we take a certain point of view about others and the world, we are forced to defend it, which is highly energy and time consuming. Every day, we can observe this not just with us, but also in companies, with politicians and celebrities. They constantly defend a certain point of view they are expected to have because their success or wealth depends on an image others have of them. They give more importance to an image they want others to have of them than to being fully alive in the moment, which *enslaves* them to their own opinions and the ones of others. For example, when forming an opinion about being successful, even if we do so just for ourselves, we would feel the need to tell everyone about our successes and try to hide any kind of failures. If we did not claim to be successful, we would not have to do that. The same would be true if we claimed we were beautiful. In that case, we would need to look great in every public appearance and picture and spend time and money retouching the latter. Holding on to an image when life's nature is to constantly change and unfold anew means we constantly go against the flow, scatter our energy, and hence, suffer.

We assume we have to defend ourselves because the offender has made an *evil* plan against us. What actually happens, though, is everybody is so self-obsessed only minding his or her own business and hurting others unintentionally. Think about all the circumstances, in which you hurt other people. In most of the cases, was it that you had the plan to intentionally hurt them or was it rather that you did something in your self-interest and you hurt them without even being aware of it beforehand? If you think the world and others are against you, then I invite you to think again.

We defend ourselves because we think what we are can be offended, without ever really looking at what it is that actually gets hurt. What if we can never get hurt, but something different from us is hurt instead; and out of habitual behavior, we identify with it? I invite you to entertain the possibility that we never get hurt in actuality. There are feelings and thoughts of hurtfulness, but they come and go like the clouds in the sky, the latter never being touched by the clouds, no matter how dark or big they are. We are afraid of bad weather not being aware that it never leaves any traces in the sky. True freedom means not only to not get offended, but also that there is not even the possibility of being offended, because there is no separate entity present to be hurt in the first place. This makes defending ourselves redundant. An offense can only occur if we give meaning to an action and declare it as an offense against us. Most of the times, it seems we do not have that option because we are not aware of this mechanism and do not understand that what puts us down is not the offense, but our defense.

Energetically speaking, during an offense the offender is trying to get the receiver into the same energy he is in. The offender finds some first relief in bringing the receiver down to his level, because in that very moment, the reaction justifies his emotional breakout. As soon as we react to the offense in any way, we also enter the same energetic downward spiral. To stay centered in our energy, it is enough not to energetically react to what is happening. Funnily enough, this is also the most powerful way to show true compassion because we cannot be there for others when being down ourselves.

Just like a brand, an image of ourselves does not have a life in itself, and hence, needs constant activities, repetition and defense to remain in the head of others. We see ourselves partly as an image and are similarly busy with constantly building and defending it. But what we are is not an image, and therefore, there is no need to ever defend an image. It is enough to see that there are as many truths as there are people out there and that what we are will always remain untouched. Being aware of this saves us much time and energy, which we can then use to express our creativity, compassion and joy. Becoming aware of the described mechanisms above, ideally also during the moment they occur, is the first and most essential step towards seeing that we are already invincible. What we are is prior to everything and never requires any effort to blossom.

What image do you have of yourself? Is it in line with the image others have of you? Why or why not?

Observe when you feel the impulse to defend your self-image in certain situations. What exactly are you trying to protect?

SPACE FOR INSPIRATION & CREATIVITY

MYTH 7 – I HAVE FREE WILL

A man can do what he wants, but not want what he wants.
– Arthur Schopenhauer, born in1788

What we believe or seemingly experience to be true

Not only do we think we are free, but it also feels as if we were able to think and choose independently. We can think whatever we want, meet the people we want, get married if we want, have a child if we want and lift our arm whenever and however we want. This to us is proof enough to think we have free will. We believe that somewhere within us – nobody really knows where exactly – there is a control center, from which we operate our thinking and doing.

As a consequence of having free will, it is important to us whether or not we are on the right path, because we have endless options to choose from at any given moment. We feel we waste our life when we are stuck in the wrong job, married to the wrong person or hang out with the wrong people. When not following the news about certain people or events, we have this underlying fear of potentially missing out on something important. Therefore, we feel pressured to continuously look for further and better options in the areas that matter to us.

What may actually be happening

Let's start by taking a closer look at how much control we have over thoughts. Thoughts stream almost constantly. Out of the around 70,000 thoughts we think every day, there are certain thoughts we interfere with or resist, and, as a consequence, they stay longer. But eventually all thoughts leave again, just like the clouds in the sky. So far, this may sound fairly logical and in line with what we know. But now, we are taking this a step further. We usually think it is us who produce those passing thoughts, that is, we assume we are the thinker of thoughts. But if this were really the case, wouldn't we choose to only think the thoughts we want, that is, only beautiful, inspiring and uplifting ones? Or maybe even better sometimes, wouldn't we also be able to decide to stop thinking altogether? Furthermore, we would know what we think or say in ten seconds from now or tomorrow at three o'clock. Does this apply to you? In this context, we are not primarily interested in whether or not it would be possible to stop thinking for a certain amount of time, but in the relationship we have with thoughts per se and in how much control we have over them in our everyday life.

On the one hand, when looking at our body and mind functions, we usually believe we are in control of what we think, what we say and what we do with our body. On the other hand, we think we are *not* in control of the heartbeat, breath, feelings, digestion, hair growth, etc., that is, most or all other body and brain functions – although there may be some *ultra-spiritual* people out there claiming to be able to do so. When claiming the latter, we do not see the big picture, but only look at very isolated events such as being able to regulate the heartbeat when focusing on it. But this does not make us the controller of the heartbeat because it beats whether we focus on it or not. Imagine for a moment someone getting frustrated because he has not been performing very well in growing his hair in the past few weeks, and therefore, would go and see a psychologist or a coach to improve. Although it may sound ridiculous, we apply this when it comes to thoughts. How many books are there about how to think more positively or how to manifest anything we want using our thoughts?

We, identified as body-mind, do not have free will. Nevertheless, it seemingly feels as if we did because the nature of the illusionary reference point – which we identify with – is to claim everything that is happening *to us*. If we see this clearly in our life, this has the power to completely change everything for the good. Concretely, what happens is the following: we notice a thought and a split second after, the mind-constructed reference point *claims* to be the one thinking the thought. This claiming does not come from an actual separate entity, but is no more than yet another thought. What is occurring here is similar to when ancient tribes or people from certain religions personify natural forces. When we are not used to this, that is, when we are able to see this from an *outside* perspective, we may think this is gullible. But when we are *in* it, we would be offended when someone told us we were making this up. The same way the ancient tribes think it were impossible to have rain without a rainmaker, we think it were impossible to have thoughts without a thinker. The existence of thoughts alone is proof enough to us to think there also must be one thinking the thought.

Another aspect invalidating the concept of free will is that there is no reference center or self that could be responsible for being in control in the first place. Not only can we see this using our own experience, but also more and more neuroscientists are discovering the same when researching the brain in its depth.

Let's exemplify how much control we have by looking at the decision-making process. As opposed to our belief, we are not the one making any decisions. Why is that? In every decision-making process, there are at least two alternatives showing up in our thoughts. More and more thoughts about the two alternatives appear. But we do not have any control whatsoever over which thoughts do or do not appear, although we may claim such control afterwards. Yet, other thoughts appear supporting option one and again other thoughts supporting option two. Further down the process, all of us have different tendencies of how we seemingly make decisions; on the one hand, we may hesitate, and on the other hand, we may not think so much about the decision. Also, we may either look at all the pros and cons in detail or not; or we either take much risk or are rather careful – we even do not have any control over any of this either. It is also not in our control how other people close to us decided about a similar matter in the past, which probably has an impact on the decision as well; or which of our friends would be available to advise us. None of that is in our control. So, looking at the decision-making process, we do not have any influence over any of the influencing factors. In a way, we could say the decision *makes itself* throughout the entire process. There is not an *I* or a *self* making the decision. Only afterwards, it claims to be the one responsible for it, which again only happens within the realm of thoughts.

While we are never the ones deciding anything, we seem to have some kind of indirect co-determination of whether our body-mind is mainly driven by other-directed or *universe-determined* factors. In the realm of the body-mind, we could say we are mostly other-directed versus universe-determined, many times without being aware of it. Other-directed means we are heavily conditioned by our culture, language, beliefs, upbringing, experiences and memories. All of those factors are driving us throughout the day and can be seen as programs that determine what we do. The less we are aware of them, the stronger they seem to work on us. For instance, I used to have the behavioral pattern of strongly adjusting to certain people in power and to rules, which made it very easy for others to *use* me to perform certain tasks or projects for them. But once I became aware of this pattern, I was *immune* to obeying and being *exploited* by strong people.

The opposite of other-directed is *universe-determined.* This means we are driven by some kind of universal intelligence, which, for example, is responsible for making trees and human beings grow, winds blow, waves move and the sun rise. It is that power or force that makes digestion work, hair grow, brains work and thoughts aware. It is an intelligence that is far higher than we will ever be able to comprehend with our mind. Therefore, the more our body-mind is universe-determined, the more light-hearted our days go by.

So, what are the consequences of not having free will in our everyday life? Does this automatically mean our destiny is predetermined? Does it mean life is hopeless because life is bad and we cannot change anything anyway? Or does it mean life is just like a movie and we can lean back and watch the show? It means we no longer have to worry about whether we are with the wrong people in the wrong place at the wrong time. There is no longer the desire to do anything other than what we are doing at any given moment. One of the biggest reasons for our suffering is namely that: the belief we could be doing something different from what we are doing at this moment. What does such an attitude do to you? See it for yourself. Do not wait for others to tell you. And do not try to find out about it by creating more theories or comparing them to others.

Having no control means we can finally rest and see things the way they are! The horses are finally in front of the carriage. We are not referring to the kind of rest we usually think of, that is, lazily lying around on the couch. Resting means not having to worry about something that is not happening and not to be causelessly afraid or shocked several times a day. It means to find true peace within and not to be disturbed by any thoughts or anything else going on in life. It finally allows us to see and fully be with what is around us, to see the bigger picture in life – not just when we are on our own, but also while we speak to others, look into each other's eyes and interact with each other. Resting means to be fully present in whatever we find ourselves doing and to fully show up to what life is presenting.

What makes you believe that you are the thinker of your thoughts and the doer of your actions?

Surrender completely to the moment and observe whether life still continues even without any of your seeming control or interference!

SPACE FOR INSPIRATION & CREATIVITY

MYTH 8 – DEATH IS SOMETHING I NEED TO BE AFRAID OF

Therefore, foolish is the man who says that he fears death, not because it will cause pain when it arrives but because anticipation of it is painful.
– Epicurus, born in 341 BC

What we believe or seemingly experience to be true

One way or another, most of us are afraid of death. We are scared that one day everything will be over. Whenever someone close to us dies, people give us the impression something really bad happened, which makes us believe death is something negative. During those moments, we often become afraid of our own death, but try to push those thoughts and feelings away. Knowing that everything that is born will also die, we think we die because our bodies were born one day.

Some of us have such a hard time dealing with a death of someone close to us that we even become depressed. In such case, we may experience an immense amount of grief, which no longer allows us to lead a light-hearted life. In a way, it seems as if society even expected us to feel down when experiencing a death of a close one.

What may actually be happening

There is no need to be afraid of death because it is part of the natural flow of life; just the way birth is, too. It is neither a disaster nor does it mean the end. It is only due to our tradition and cultural conditioning that we do not celebrate both, birth and death, in the same manner.

Although we do *celebrate* death in Western society, it takes place in a rather low-spirited atmosphere than in a light-hearted one. There is nothing wrong with feeling sad when someone close to us passes away, but it is not very healthy, neither on a societal nor individual level, to not accept it and to make it look as if a disaster happened. It is essential to see that the event itself is never a tragedy, but the meaning we give to it, usually is. In other words, the event of dying and the grief that comes with it are essentially unrelated. It only appears to be related due to our conditioning of never having questioned it in its very essence. The purpose here is not to disregard, play down or ignore death, but to understand what it truly is, and at the same time, to see that we are free from it.

From the body-mind perspective, when we die, it seems as if the world and everyone else died with us. Similarly, before the body was born, the world did not seem to exist separate from us, yet, but it only came into existence through the birth of the body. In the same way, we also think the world does not exist anymore – at least for us – when the body passes away. This not only applies to death, but also to life. The world only seemingly exists in dependency of our body, or strictly speaking, the world and the body only exist in dependency of our formless awareness. Or have we ever experienced the world without our body being present, or without being aware of our experience? Based on our experience, this is not possible. Everybody and everything we are aware of is happening within our awareness, not outside or separate from it, which has tremendous implications on our life. It gives us all the power, not only over us, but also over others and the entire world – not just *some* power over *some* people and events, but *all* the power. To us, other people only exist as long as we exist. If we did not exist, they would no longer exist to us. The same is true for everything in the world and even the world itself. Furthermore, this means we are the ones giving *everything all* the meaning it has, because nothing has an inherent meaning. So, our partner, all of your friends and all celebrities are only what we allow them to be. See for yourself if the people around you are generous and open-minded, or instead, filled with hate, aggression or fear. You are the one giving them the meaning they have. Not anybody else out there. And what kind of world do you live in? Is it a world, in which people are kind to each other or is it a world full of conflicts? What meaning do you give to the world, others and yourself?

Let's take a closer look at what happens when we are afraid of death. Death only concerns the body-mind structure, but never touches what we are. Since we usually assume consciousness is a function of the brain or body, we think after the death of the body-mind, consciousness also no longer exists. However, it is the other way around, that is, our body and brain appear *in* awareness or consciousness. To discover this, we do not have to believe scientists or anyone else, but can see it for ourselves. We would never be able to perceive our bodies or thoughts if we were made of that very same substance, just as if our tongue were made of salt and we eat salt, we would not be able to taste it. Taking a body-camera analogy, assuming our body was a camera, we would not be the camera, but the one behind looking through the camera. What we are can never be the camera itself or anything seen in front of the camera. In the same way, during the act of dying, which, by the way, does not represent the end of what we are, but the end of the body-mind, the *juice* leaves the body, but it does not affect us, that is, the one behind the camera in any way. Yet, as long as we identify as the body-mind, that is the camera, we will constantly be afraid of death, in one way or another. We usually never question whether we are our body because the idea seems ridiculous to most of us. If we are not yet open to entertain that possibility, we often do become more open to this when we experience a death of a close friend, become ill, lose something that was precious to us or go through another life-changing event.

The point is that once we come to a living understanding of not being the body, it won't even be possible to be afraid of death or anything else anymore, by nature. It just won't be possible, because what we are can never die. In this case, we also do not have to go to see a therapist, pray, do rituals or find other ways to cope with fear. Again, this is no theoretical or absurd discussion or conspiracy, but all of us can use our own mundane experience to entertain the possibility that this is what is actually happening.

If we were really our bodies, we would most likely live in a completely different manner. We would be totally scared by every step we take. If really everything came to an end through the death of the body, we would never take the risks in life we usually do. We would not engage in bungee jumping or similar adventures, but would rather be in constant fear, or at least have an underlying fear of getting sick or die. Instead, there is something telling us that everything is good, no matter what. This message comes right from what we are, that is, from what is behind the camera.

When we talk to people who are afraid of death – mostly people who have not given this matter much challenging thought – they usually share the belief of the masses, that is, that we die with the body one day. But when speaking to people who went through near-death experiences or have a living understanding of what we are, we hear we are *something* beyond the body. Instead of believing either one of those parties, find out the answer for yourself, without being influenced by your upbringing and what other people tell you.

Inherently, death is neither good nor bad. Again, if it is true that we give everything all the meaning it has, we give death its meaning, too. Only if we were not aware of, and hence, not free from outside influences, we would give everything the meaning it has based on our conditioning and beliefs we pick up from society, our parents, teachers and friends. Hence, it is up to our degree of awareness how free we are with regard to giving meaning to death – and life.

Paradoxically, when it comes to death, we are afraid of something we will never even experience ourselves. That which is afraid, the body-mind structure, won't experience death. Once the body is dead, there won't be any thought or feeling from that body-mind about how much *it* wishes to still be alive because it already dissolved. While we, as the body-mind, do not experience our own death, the people around us do. And we are not taught how to healthily deal with such intense situations, especially, for instance, when we are young and our mother passes away. People who experience a heavy amount of grief after a death of a loved one may carry around a veil of sadness in subtle layers in their bodies, which drives their emotional world and is perceivable by others – many times, even decades after the event. With regard to how to appropriately deal with death, it is not about being mentally strong, but about understanding that dying is part of nature and that we are never that which dies. It may also help to understand that the one who dies would not wish his or her loved ones to go through a depressing time because of this.

There may be something deep inside you that resonates with what is written here, although you may not be able to fully put your mind around it. At the same time, you may notice strong thoughts telling you that this sounds like a fairy tale and that reality is different; not only highly recognized experts but even your own feeling may tell you that you are your body and die one day. Let those thoughts and feelings pass and become aware of your actual experience beyond your beliefs and see whether you can entertain the possibility that you never die. It is up to you whether you keep listening to your old beliefs or whether you are ready to jump into the realm of freedom. Nobody else can do this for you. See who you are not, and by seeing that, death and fear will no longer be a problem. By being able to discern between what we are and what we are not, we have the power to experience a life based on joy, compassion and peace while fully participating in life.

When was the very first time you were afraid of death? What exactly were you afraid of?

Which state of mind do you usually find yourself in when you are afraid of death?

SPACE FOR INSPIRATION & CREATIVITY

MYTH 9 – MY THOUGHTS ARE FROM AND ABOUT ME

Look past your thoughts,
so, you may drink the pure nectar of this moment.
– Rumi, born in 1207

What we believe or seemingly experience to be true

We inherently assume we are the thinker of *our* thoughts, the feeler of *our* feelings and the doer of *our* actions, without ever questioning it. Since we believe thoughts are about us, we are almost constantly putting our attention on the thinking process, walking around as if we were hypnotized, not really being aware of what is happening right in front of our eyes in the *here and now*.

Another consequence of claiming that *our* thoughts and actions are from and about us is that many of us tend to be shy or afraid under certain circumstances. We feel the need to protect ourselves, and at the same time, wish we were more open and authentic when interacting with others. Funnily enough, when looking at this more closely, we are not even sure what exactly we protect deep down. Furthermore, many of us have issues with matters such as privacy. Believing that thoughts and feelings are from or about us, we act as if we had to keep them private to stay safe. We are afraid that certain people might use *our* information to harm us or make money with it.

What may actually be happening

While we are the ones *noticing* thoughts, feelings and actions, we are not the ones *producing* them. We are prior, not only to thoughts, but also to the seeming entity that claims to be the thinker. What makes us overlook that we are not the thinker is partly the speed of how fast the claiming occurs, which takes place within a split second after noticing thoughts. If we were really responsible for the brain and body functions such as thinking, beating the heart and breathing, we would most likely die after a few minutes because we would forget to beat the heart, split certain cells or breathe air while talking to a friend. While thoughts are not from us, the other essential aspect in this is to see that thoughts are never about us. Thoughts can only be about the body-mind or the form, but what we are is the formless – at any given moment, even if we were convinced of the opposite.

When thoughts are not from or about us, we may wonder how we notice them and why they appear to be unique or private to us. What happens is the following: our body-mind takes the role of an *antenna* picking up different frequencies, that is, thoughts and feelings of different qualities, just as a radio antenna would do. When being in an uplifting state, the body-mind attracts uplifting thoughts and feelings and when being in a low-spirited state, we pick up low-spirited ones. In addition to those temporary moods, the body-mind vibrates at a certain base frequency unique to each body-mind depending on elements such as the beliefs and conditioning we have collected, and our level of freedom.

Therefore, while some of us tend to be calm and uplifting, others might attract problems in accordance with their lower base frequency, even when encountering the same situation. Yet, the good news is that our base frequency can easily change. And the even better news is that what we are is not the body-mind. If you will, this entire book exists to help us uplift the base frequency of the body-mind and see what we are beyond what we take ourselves to be, which allows us to experience true freedom.

Another factor playing a role in what thoughts or feelings the body-mind attracts is the environment it is in. When standing by the ocean, we usually feel calm and relaxed, also because there is not much *noise* from a so-called group mind. When participating in a seminar or walking in a shopping mall, we notice many different thoughts, and also feel rather agitated than calm. This is due to the group mind being highly active in such situations. This group mind makes us pick up thoughts and feelings together with the people around, creating a more powerful antenna, which then vibrates at the frequency of the group. Each one of us has had the experience of going to a bigger event being in a relaxed state of mind and becoming nervous without any explainable reason. Instead of being obsessed with wondering why we are nervous and trying to stay calm, it would be enough for us to recognize that the nervousness is caused by the group antenna and does not have anything to do with us as an individual body-mind. As soon as we become aware of this, we are able to stay effortlessly calm because we are aware the thoughts and feelings are not from or about us. I struggled with such situations for quite a long time and took every negative thought and nervousness as my own and started to believe that I am not a strong person in big crowds – until one day I became *immune* to it by realizing that the nervousness was not mine – which, by the way, is not to be confused with pushing away nervousness. To illustrate this further, let's take a look at an example from two friends who independently from each other experienced the same situation. They sat in their respective apartments thinking that they still have to feed the dog that day. The thought appeared to be crazy to them because they do neither own nor take care of a dog. The week after, they understood that their neighbors had bought a dog, and hence, realized they picked up the thoughts their neighbors received. I am sure many of us encounter similar examples every day, maybe without even being aware of it. Similarly, we have probably noticed that the quality of thoughts changes dependent on the location and surroundings we are in. For instance, certain people are most creative when being in nature or in the shower, which can be a valuable discovery when making a piece of art or brainstorming about an invention. This is nothing *crazy* or *esoteric*, but our actual experience every day. When putting the more subtle things of life into words, many times they sound a bit *foolish*. Again, I am not asking you to believe what is written here, but I invite you to entertain the possibility to eventually see this in your own life.

When being aware that thoughts are not from and about us, also the protection, privacy and shyness issues become redundant, or at least no longer represent a problem. We would only want to hide or feel guilty for thoughts and feelings when assuming we are their producers or owners. For example, if you knew you were not the doer while seemingly making a mistake at work, you would be completely open to share the mistake with your colleagues and manager because you would not be in need to protect your reputation or feel bad about it because it was not you making the mistake. As a consequence, you and your colleagues could directly focus on solving the problem. And as a pleasant side effect, the people around you may appreciate you for being transparent about this, which makes it even easier for them to trust you in the future. Alternatively, if you assumed to be the doer, you would struggle in many ways. Firstly, you would feel guilty for making the mistake asking yourself why you were not more careful. Secondly, you would be afraid of damaging your reputation in the company and you would even have to deal with unreasonable thoughts such as being eventually fired from your job, worried of not being able to pay your bills anymore and eventually ending up being poor. Thirdly, you would be indecisive whether or not to communicate the mistake to your manager or colleague, not being sure what would be worse: to tell others how *stupid* you are when admitting your mistake or feeling afraid of being caught when others find out about the mistake. Fourthly, due to points one to three, your whole peace of mind would be destroyed. And fifthly, the mistake would have a negative impact on the company because it is not being dealt with. We could probably go on and on with this list, which shows us how inventive we are when pretending to be the owner of something. The same mechanisms apply to issues such as privacy, shyness and embarrassment. Play it through and see it for yourself, not only when reading this, but also in the moment it happens in your life.

Interestingly, when meeting someone who speaks out embarrassing thoughts, we often resonate with her deep down because through her openness, she expresses what we do not dare to speak out ourselves. This is something many comedians use to make their audience laugh. They master the art of bringing up underlying aspects we try to hide towards others and make them public. Comedy in that sense can be seen as an entertaining form of therapy.

There are certain methods or unofficial movements stating that when feeling down, we can turn around our life by just thinking positively again. While this *fake it until we make it* tool may provide a certain amount of temporary relief, it actually systematically ignores the important and subtle messages coming from our intuition. For instance, we may pick up negative thoughts from a family member as a sign they are in need. But if we just rigorously pushed negativity away and replaced it with positivity, then, strictly speaking, it would be a form of *violence* towards life. Positive thinking as an attitude shows we are not able to deal with thoughts because we give them the power to rule our life. The solution is not to be glued to thoughts, but to allow any thought to arise, understand it is not from or about us. From that distance, we are then able to appropriately deal with the situation. No effort or methodology is required for that. This also illustrates the problem never lies in the existence of negative thoughts, but rather in us giving them the power to destroy our moment, our day or even our week. They seemingly have that power because we give it to them in the first place. When identifying with something, whose nature is to alternate between positive and negative states, our life will be characterized by the same pattern. It happens that in one moment we can be happy and in the next moment we can be depressed, not because something bad happens right in front of us, but because a certain unwanted thought comes into our awareness that most likely will never even manifest.

Not identifying with thoughts or feelings sets us free to a degree that is way beyond what we will ever be able to imagine. Being truly free enables us to put our focus more on expressing ourselves and no longer on being shy or embarrassed in public. It also enables us to reach out a hand to help people in the most appropriate way. And finally, it will allow us to rest. Becoming aware of our seeming *enslavement* to thoughts will bring a freedom that does not depend on whether there are positive or negative thoughts. The solution is right in front of us, from moment to moment. It is not enough to believe what is written here or to argue for or against it. But it is enough to see it for yourself, right now. Nobody else can do this for you.

When not trying to control or interfering with thoughts, how does the effect thoughts have on you change?

If it is true that you are not your thoughts and feelings, what then is your relationship with them?

SPACE FOR INSPIRATION & CREATIVITY

3

The world is in you

MYTH 10 – THERE IS AN OBJECTIVE WORLD OUT THERE

Do not feel lonely; the entire universe is inside you.
– Rumi, born in 1207

What we believe or seemingly experience to be true

We think there is an objective world *out there* that exists independently and separately from us. Having a reality in its own, it consists of matter, atoms, space and other particles. Not only are we separate from the world, but also from billions of other individuals, each one representing his or her own entity. Furthermore, we think there are independent events taking place whether we are there to notice them or not. We think they occur, although none of us has ever experienced anything outside of our awareness.

Since the world is objective, it appears the same to everyone and can be measured. Therefore, when discussing objects, theories or events, we can tell whether someone is right or wrong or whether one tells the truth or not by simply comparing what he or she says with what we measure.

Starting in school, life is all about learning, analyzing and better understanding this objective world using the knowledge for our own benefit, or in some instances also for the benefit of all. In our attempt to preserve and improve the knowledge of this objective world, we have structured, divided, examined and discussed every single particle on planet earth we could find so far. Experts at schools, universities, institutions and companies transfer the knowledge to students and employees in highly fragmented pieces of information. Those experts usually have an extraordinary level of expertise within their specialized fields, but do not know much about other fields or the bigger picture.

What may actually be happening

Imagine a tree was falling in a forest and nobody is around – neither any human, animal nor any recording device such as a video camera or microphone with the ability to perceive or record anything. Would there be a sound? A person with a conventional perspective would say *Of course, there is a sound because there is an objective reality out there*. But is there really a sound? While the ultimate answer would be *We do not know*, the plausible answer would be *No* when simply relying on our own experience. We have never heard a sound from a falling tree when we were not there observing the event. So, based on our own experience, that is, first-hand information, there is no sound when the tree is falling.

In a way, the different answers to this imaginary experiment beautifully reflect what we value in society. On the one hand, we can observe a strong focus on second-hand knowledge or speculation, that is, believing what we hear from so-called experts while ignoring our own experience. This approach is highly valued by society and reinforces our daily behavior, for which we are rewarded at school and at work. On the other hand, our first-hand experience builds the basis for being able to think on our own. While the latter is not valued by any formal reward system, it plays an essential role in not being afraid to be different from the rest or from what is written in textbooks. The interesting point here is not so much whether or not the answer to the tree falling is *yes* or *no*, but rather *how* we come to our respective answers and how we build our reality in any given situation in general.

As opposed to the common belief that reality is something we can find somewhere *out there*, it never exists separate from us. We are the ones bringing it into the world. Or put another way: we are not in the world, but the world is in us. If an objective world really existed, each one of us would agree on everything out there because there would be no room for any kind of disagreement – without exception. But is this in line with what we actually observe every day? Do we see more agreement or disagreement? It is only possible to disagree with each other when each one of us brings a different reality into the world. We know from our own experience, which, by the way, is also backed up by discoveries in quantum physics, that the observer has the biggest influence on what is happening in any given experiment or event. Just because our parents told us that we were born into a preexisting world one day, it does not necessarily mean this is true; in the same way, many other aspects our parents tell us are just things they picked up from their parents and environment passing those on to us without having ever profoundly challenged them. Approaching life based on second-hand information restricts us in many ways and makes us prone to manipulation without even realizing it. Maybe it is time to entertain the possibility that the world, together with all the people, objects, thoughts, feelings and events, is born within us every morning when waking up – *us* obviously not meaning the body, but our formless awareness. We are the ones bringing everyone and everything to life. And that, which is alive, is what all of us have in common. But again, it is not about believing or not believing our parents or what is written here, but about figuring out who we are using first-hand information. Also, I invite you not to try to put your thoughts around what you are reading here. If you try to understand this with what you already know, it won't take you anywhere, but rather make you resist. It is enough to stay open-minded. Simply take a moment during your daily activities and see if there is any possibility that what is written here may also be your experience.

To illustrate how we bring reality into the world, let's take a look at a movie theater analogy. The main elements of the movie theater we are looking at are the images appearing on the screen and the projector. All the movie action including the stories, scenes, arguments, thoughts and emotions are projected onto the screen in form of images; sound and other elements usually also play a role, but we are ignoring those for simplicity reasons. Translated into our reality, the moving images appearing on the screen represent the world of form, that is, everything we are able to perceive through our senses including objects, people, feelings, thoughts and subtle energies. When it comes to our identity, we usually believe we are one of the characters appearing on the screen. The element bringing everything to life, that is, making the objects visible on the screen, is the white light of the projector, which is outside of the movie, or the form. This white light represents the formless in our realm of reality, which is what we are at all times. Without it, none of the images of the movie would be visible. Similarly, without us, the world would not exist. What we are is not something appearing on the screen within the movie, but the light of awareness, out of which all form appears. In this context, none of the characters of the movie or none of the form in the world has a reality on its own. This is similar to the activity of dreaming. The only entity that exists in a dream context is the dreamer, and without him or her, the dream including all its dream characters and objects would not exist.

Further looking at how we perceive the world, we usually assume the body itself is the one seeing, hearing and generally perceiving objects. But this is not the case. The body is not the subject, but an object that can be perceived. By default, that which perceives – the subject – has to be different from that which it perceives – the object; in the same way, a tongue made of salt cannot taste salt. What we are is not perceivable, and hence, one cannot label us, see us, hear us, agree or disagree with us or discuss about us. Similarly, when we see a beautiful sunset over the ocean, it is not the sunset or ocean that is intrinsically beautiful, but we are merely reminded of our own beauty, which is mirrored by the sunset. The cause for most of our problems is that we start from the wrong starting point mistaking the object for the subject, which makes us prone to pain in the first place.

Our beliefs and conditioning also strongly contribute to how we perceive life, and whether we are pro or contra a certain political party, tennis player, country, religion or way of living. It is as if we saw the world through a pair of glasses made of beliefs. For instance, they determine whether or not we have prejudices against certain people, what kind of people are able to provoke us and what disappoints us. This conditioning already starts in the womb. The younger we are, the more directly we soak in everything from our environment, especially the conditioning coming from our parents in form of thoughts, feelings and actions. Most of the time, the meaning we give to everything is determined by our conditioning, which is a state comparable to being in an *autopilot mode*. Essentially, this also means that people, political parties, religions and situations are never good or bad per se, but only what meaning we give to them. By being more aware of the mechanisms of how we create reality, we are able to be less judgmental about people, which enables us to rather connect with their essence and not with an image we may have of them.

As a consequence of us bringing reality into the world, there is also no such thing as right and wrong. Yet, when looking around us, we see innumerable conflicts in this world over this. Everybody wants to be right, even to such a degree that they are willing to go to court or to war for that. For instance, when someone approaches us saying we do not do a good enough job, we usually become agitated and defensive because we want him to know the truth, that is, that we are doing a good job, not being aware that what he said does neither have anything to do with the truth nor with us. This can only become a problem if we are attached to what other people think.

The same is true when supporting politicians. Let's say someone supported a politician's decision to let refugees come into a particular country. If she now heard someone expressing an opinion going against hers, she would think it is important to stand up for her point of view or the truth and enlighten or go against the other person. This would only make sense if there were an objective truth or reality *out there* – or of course, if we tried to intentionally manipulate someone. But the point is, there is no such thing as the one and only truth out there. Hence, the good news is that we do not have to waste our energy trying to enlighten other people. We do not have to convince others about anything in this world; whether it is about our friends, the world overall or us. We do not have to change others and what they think of anyone or anything. The more we try to do so, the more we lose ourselves in a low-spirited energy that not only hurts us, but also the people around.

Nonetheless, it seems as if certain authorities gave us the impression that they have monopolized the truth, which most of us buy into without being aware of it. Governments, institutions, corporations or media companies pretend there is an official worldview that needs to be adopted by everyone, or at least by the ones who want to be accepted by society. Galileo's story from a few hundred years ago, which is mentioned in the *Overture* of this book, is a good example for how this attempt to monopolize the truth works. Everybody who thinks differently from a commonly accepted worldview, especially if it represents a threat to the current one, may be accused of creating conspiracy theories. As a result, many of us do not dare to freely express our thoughts in front of certain people or in public because we are afraid of being judged as *different* or *crazy*.

Seeing that we are not in the world, but the world is in us has an immense impact on how we spend our days. We would see that instead of primarily learning about mathematics, law and geography, all of us, especially children, would benefit far more from learning about who we are. The magic lies neither in matter nor in theories, but in the very essence of what we are made of. By understanding who we truly are, other people, institutions and events lose their seeming power over whether we are having a good or a bad day. Furthermore, we come to realize that life is full of joy, compassion and light-heartedness. We finally feel whole again, independent of what happens around us and we no longer have the feeling of always missing out on something. It allows us to see the perfection of life even in the light of duality, that is, in the good and the bad, in happiness and misery, or in war and peace. We no longer get distracted by the *noise*, but are rooted in our never-changing light, recognizing the divine play that takes place within us.

Looking at the most profound changes in your life, is it the situations that have changed or rather your perspective on them? Elaborate.

Does the world exist to you even if you were not aware of it?

SPACE FOR INSPIRATION & CREATIVITY

MYTH 11 – MEDIA PAINTS AN OBJECTIVE PICTURE OF THE WORLD

Those who are able to see beyond the shadows and lies of their culture will never be understood, let alone believed, by the masses.
– Plato, born in 427 BC

What we believe or seemingly experience to be true

Every day we follow news from various traditional, alternative and social media channels to be informed about what is happening in the world. We hear or read mostly about negative stories making us feel low, fearful or rather serious, which in turn gives us the impression that, all in all, the world is cold and unfair. At the same time, it is subtly conveyed that as long as we stick to certain rules and listen to advice from the so-called experts featured in media, we have a good chance to live a safe and decent life.

Furthermore, we do not really see the need to challenge the content of well-known media outlets because we perceive them as more or less credible due to their awareness level, reputation and professional appearance.

In a way, it seems as if we could not even live without media. This is partly due to the following reasons: first of all, we assume there is an objective, separate world *out there*. And, since we cannot be everywhere at once and want to stay informed about what is happening in the world, we feel the need to follow all noteworthy stories. Secondly, we want to be aware of important affairs because it enables us to engage in small talk with our colleagues and friends, who else may judge us for not knowing essential happenings in our society. Thirdly, we look for some kind of reference to compare us to the general public to see how we are doing versus others in life. It is important for us to be in line with the latest trends and state-of-the-art knowledge – whether this may be in fashion, business, sports, personal development or any other field of interest or what we consider to be important. We somehow want to fit in and not be considered an outcast, especially by people we look up to or care about.

When scrolling through social media sites, we get the impression our friends lead amazing lives, almost as if they were celebrities. Compared to ours, everyone else's life looks much more attractive, which sometimes makes us feel lonely and jealous.

What may actually be happening

Let's start by briefly taking a look at whether the three reasons from above about our obsession with media are justified or not.

First of all, there is no objective world, which is described in more detail under *Myth 10*. This means media are not about reporting facts or neutrally informing about current affairs, but rather about storytelling – for the simple reason that there are never any events happening outside of us. What may appear as a surprise or even as a shock to some is something we can easily follow when looking at it more closely using our own mundane experience. Understanding this can have a big impact on how we experience life overall. Since there is no objective world, it implies that journalists or managers of media companies give everything in the world all the meaning it has because the world and other people do not have any intrinsic reality. So, what we watch and see in media every day are fabricated stories told by a few powerful companies that have the rather complex task of pleasing their lobbyists. *Fabricated* does not always necessarily mean the people at media companies want to intentionally harm others, but it means that the content is not about objective facts, but about stories. And most importantly, in our role as the final instance, it is us who give even that content all the meaning it has.

Secondly, it is impossible for us to ever miss out on something. If we assume a separate world exists, we automatically get the impression it is possible to miss out on events, people or other exciting or important affairs. Yet, the events we think we could miss actually never happen according to our first-hand experience. If at all, they are only imaginary taking place in form of thoughts, stories or images in combination with feelings. If it were possible to ever miss out on something, life would represent a constant struggle because we would miss out on zillions of events at any given moment. Just imagine how many stunning locations, concerts, sunny beaches, beautiful mountains and like-minded people we would be missing out on right now. If information or certain people are meant to reach us, they will. We never have to be afraid of missing out on anything.

Thirdly, there is no a need for us to adjust to others or the world. On the contrary, it is more appropriate for us and even for everyone around to let the world and others adjust to us. The more authentic we are, the more we attract other authentic people into our life. In contrast, the more we try to fit in, the more life becomes a struggle and the more we have to pay attention to everything happening in the world. So, it is okay not to feel pressured to think we have to follow trends, state-of-the-art knowledge or ways on how to become successful. Everything we need to know is either within or right in front of us at any given moment.

To get a feel for questioning the status quo, I invite you to use your first-hand experience. See for yourself how you feel before, during and after reading or watching the news, and how, in contrast, you feel when not consuming media for a few days. Observe how it actually makes you feel. Which one of the two gives or takes away energy? What thoughts and feelings do you experience? Do you feel uplifted or low-spirited? Do not wait for someone to tell you how it might be, but experience it yourself. As opposed to the low-spirited feeling I get from following the news, what I see in life every day is mostly positive. Based on my experience, the picture of the world media *paint* and the world I perceive are different like night and day. How is it for you?

In the following paragraphs, we will discover how media impact the way we create and perceive reality. Given there is no objective world, media convey an image of the world according to what they think is right or what they want their audience to believe. On closer inspection of the internal and external structures of media companies, we quickly come to the understanding that there are many people, organizations, parties, lobbyists and companies that have their own agendas, for which media serves as a powerful megaphone to influence the masses. At the same time, it is noteworthy that in most countries, media companies are owned and controlled either by governments and politicians – which, for instance, is the case in Italy – or by large, profit-driven private corporations – which, for example, is the case in the United States. Since the beginning of printing and broadcasting, rulers have been aware of the power of spreading the word to the masses and how easy it is to make people believe virtually any message coming from an acknowledged source. Nowadays, a few global and regional press agencies spread the messages about all major global affairs to newspapers and TV stations. This makes it easy for them to create a consistency in what different media outlets report around the world, giving us the impression that the content must be correct, since many media companies, even from different countries, report the same stories. Importantly, the power of media lies not only in how they interpret particular life events, but especially in the choice of which events they report about on a consistent basis. Do they cover stories that make us feel fearful or rather uplifting? At the same time, I am sure most people working in media have good intentions and are interested in telling the audience stories that are as close as possible to how they perceive the particular events, while still fitting them to the current accepted worldview and most likely also to the interests of the owners of the media company. The point here is neither to go against media in any form nor to create any conspiracy theories, but to raise awareness of what role media play in building reality.

Media even have the power to create our reality, if we allow it to happen – which we usually do without being aware of it, no matter how intelligent we might think we are. Imagine you read and hear that you are going to be the next winner of the Nobel Peace Prize from ten different, credible sources that all appear in a highly professional manner. You hear this message every day for many months and at some stage even directly from your friends. The first few days and weeks you would probably feel a bit awkward because you know you have not contributed in any noteworthy way to world peace, but the longer this went on, the more you would start to believe it and would even come up with reasons why you would actually be the right nominee. It may even influence your behavior in a way that you would start engaging in helping others or even join a foundation. It would not take long for it to become a living reality for you without even having to think about it anymore. This is how media – together with our parents, teachers, etc. – have conditioned us with regard to the image we have about the world and about us. It appears as if we were hypnotized by the daily repetition coming from different information sources. When we give the news the power to tell us what reality is, we let others create reality for us. Yet, the problem is not the news per se, but us seemingly giving others and the media the power to shape our reality – without even being aware of it. For a moment, try to forget everything you have ever heard through media. How would your image of the world be different than the one you have now? Take a moment and let the answer take effect on you.

Understanding how media and companies use credibility to make people believe them is essential in order not to be deceived. Besides the already mentioned credibility elements, repetition and the consistency of what is being reported by various different sources are some of the most powerful tools to make people believe almost everything. It is already enough if several media outlets, our friends and people we know repeat the very same message. That way, inevitably, the image media present to us about the world and its affairs becomes our seeming reality. This knowledge about how to use credibility to influence the masses is also applied in marketing and any other mass communication. Put in very simple terms, it works as follows: if hearing a message from an unknown source, we are usually skeptical. If hearing it from a known and trusted source, we tend to believe it without hesitation. If it comes from a source we do not really know, but is linked to certain recognized people we *know*, we do not question the message either; which, by the way, is a strategy used in credentialing marketing, that is, marketing with celebrities. And if hearing the same message from different sources, we think it would almost be a crime not to believe it. Not believing such messages would make us look as if we were members of a *conspiracy theory club*. Media companies and brands with the highest credibility to us are usually the ones our parents already trusted. Subliminally, we also assume if a particular media outlet were the *bad guy*, everyone else would have already found out about them. But we all know from experience that there have been countless cases, in which everybody believed someone was the *good guy*, but he or she turned out to be the *bad guy*.

Even on an energetic level, media have an immense impact on us. For instance, in my teenage years, I frequently listened to the radio in the car. When the news was on, I never felt good without being fully aware of it. My intuition told me to no longer listen to it, but my thoughts were stronger and convinced me to continue to do so every day to be informed about important events and affairs. Since following the news is seen as something well-educated people do, I indirectly felt pressured by my parents, teachers and society to follow them. When I became more sensitive to what gives me and takes away energy, I immediately stopped consuming media because I clearly noticed it strongly takes away energy. Nowadays, when I happen to listen to the radio in rare occasions, I clearly feel how my mood or frequency level drops – and it seems as if I enter a state of hypnosis. What is your experience? I invite you to observe it the next time you consume media.

Another phenomenon linked to media is their power to direct the attention of the masses to specific affairs, which again shapes how we perceive reality. In a way, our attention is glued to the topics and values media or their influencers dictate, and hence, affairs only become problems or scandals to the masses once they are covered in various media outlets over a long enough period of time. All other affairs in the world, many of them even of bigger impact to us, may never come to our attention because they are either not covered at all or not enough by media. The more we are exposed to certain stories, images and messages, the more we perceive the world based on those very impressions, which in mass media today are mostly negative. Just imagine how our perception of the world would drastically change, if mass media and advertising mainly presented the countless amazing stories about life that happen nonstop. Similarly, we only become aware of the status quo and start challenging it when we hear about substantial changes in the system, such as a breakdown of the financial markets, natural disasters, an explosion of a nuclear plant and so on. We hardly ever challenge the status quo without there being a scandal, yet, although there may already be many signs showing that the current system has already failed. We have lost the ability to challenge the status quo independently from whether it may be a hot topic in media or not. At the same time, we are never the victim of anything or anybody, and in the same way, media are only as powerful as we allow them to be. Since we allow them to be extremely powerful, they have us in their grip.

Let's take a look at what impact media have on us by looking at a concrete example, such as a terrorist attack. In such an event, media serve as an outlet to the original source of the message, which, for instance, could come from the public relations department of one of the national secret services. After a bombing, one of the secret services claiming to have a message from so-called terrorists sends out an official statement that was cleared beforehand by some acknowledged authorities, such as governments. Once that statement reaches the press agencies, TV stations and newspapers, they report about the motives and the people behind the bombings, without being able to check the authenticity of the information, blindly trusting the source. The credibility point described above also applies to the relationship of media to governments, that is, media would trust credible governments without any hesitation forgetting that in many instances, the people from the source usually have certain hidden agendas. On our side, we believe what is written in the newspapers without hesitation, and as a consequence, we condemn certain groups or people, argue with friends and colleagues in all seriousness, although none of us actually knows what is really going on behind or even in front of the curtains. This is gossiping at its best, no matter how sophisticated or serious some of us pretend to be. We all have the same information available and take a certain standpoint based on our beliefs and conditioning. Although nobody really knows what is going on, everyone believes he or she has to say something very smart. For us, the gossiping is not so much about the particular topic, but more about building our self-worth through those discussions. It would be the easiest thing on earth to fool the masses about global events as such, if one intended to do so. We have become so used to trusting second-hand information that we have forgotten how to question things, especially when it comes from seemingly recognized authorities. It is hard to get fooled when we only trust first-hand information, that is, something we experience ourselves. And even in this case, we may not be able to believe what we seemingly experience because many of us are not aware of our deep conditioning, which make us experience events differently from what is actually happening.

Those of us who have been featured in media themselves may be aware of the discrepancy of how we usually experience a particular situation ourselves and how it is later presented in media. Many times, journalists reported about my life on the tennis court or about awards I have received. There was almost always a huge discrepancy between what I experienced and what was reported; it felt as if there had been two different events taking place, despite the journalists not having any bad intentions. They just saw it very differently because they gave it their meaning and also had the agenda to write the article as interesting as possible for their readers to attract more clients. Most often, the articles were strongly exaggerated, just like all the press releases we wrote about the products we marketed in the companies I worked for.

What also shapes our image about the world and us is social media. Scrolling through social media platforms gives us the impression our life is boring and we are not very attractive because there are always people out there who are more beautiful, have more likes on their posts and videos, are more successful, travel more, have more money and go to cooler parties than we do. The mechanism behind this works as follows: our conventional self-image can be seen as a puzzle, each piece representing repetitive or strong thoughts, emotions and occurrences triggering the meaning we give to our body-mind named Benjamin, for instance. Since we are the only one being aware of all those unfiltered thoughts, feelings and occurrences that happened to this particular body-mind, including all the great, embarrassing, beautiful and not so beautiful moments, our self-image tends to be worse than the one others have about us. The closer we are to certain people, the more similar our image about them is to the one we have about us because we also see them in favorable and not so favorable moments. With regard to the people we are not very close to, our image consists of adding up the few impressions we have about them, which are usually mostly from favorable situations, which results in us having a great image about them. Since they perceive us from the same distance we perceive them, they also have a great image about us. When it comes to the image we have about celebrities, the puzzle consists of mostly impressive pieces because they adorn themselves with the crème de la crème stylists, wardrobes, cars, houses and only present themselves in professionally retouched images and videos, which is all we see from them. Their agents intentionally create a *fairy tale-like world* around them. The image we have about celebrities and the image they have about themselves are far from one another. Funnily enough, though, many of us desire to become a celebrity one day, not being aware that nothing on the fundamental level would change for us. This desire is reinforced every day because we usually care more about what other people think of us than how we actually feel.

Overall, it can be *dangerous* to think we are aware of something, when actually we are not. I have met many people who would answer with *no* when asked whether they believe what media say. But in the very moment they are consuming media and are talking about a certain topic in all seriousness, they are no longer aware they actually do. The point here is that it is not enough to be aware of something intellectually, but in the very moment something occurs. That way, we are able to change what we are seemingly *in*. But when we are not aware, it appears to have the power to control us.

At the end of the day, this chapter is not about whether or not we should follow the news, but about clearly seeing how easy it is for others to direct our attention to certain affairs and to deceive us if we are not aware of how reality is created. However, when being aware of the mechanisms, the choice is with us. We are then free to decide whether or not we want to be exposed to negativity every day and in what areas we want to challenge the status quo. To be free from being manipulated represents a breakthrough. While finally being able to think on our own and becoming more and more autonomous in our way of living, we are also able to be truly compassionate. As a result, life as such appears to be significantly more lighthearted in everything we do and our relationships appear to be richer.

In what way has media influenced the image you have of yourself and the world?

Is it possible to have an innocent image of the world even when consuming media every day? Why or why not?

SPACE FOR INSPIRATION & CREATIVITY

MYTH 12 – PRESSURE COMES FROM OTHERS

Live within; be not shaken by outward happenings.
– Aurobindo, born in 1872

What we believe or seemingly experience to be true

All of us are under some kind of pressure in life. This could be the pressure to have enough money, to perform well in a job, to meet a significant other, to be accepted by peers, to raise a child in the best possible way or to deal with life in general. We take it for granted that pressure is part of everyday life and act as if it came from the *outside*, that is, from our manager, parents, friends and society. Subliminally, we think life would be much easier and more peaceful if others were not so demanding.

Just as it is the case with most other life skills, nobody teaches us how to effectively deal with pressure. Instead of understanding its cause and what it really is, we jump right into looking for ways to deal with its symptoms by fabricating a comfort zone around it, which, at the same time, means making sacrifices. For instance, we may deal with pressure by avoiding certain situations or people that trigger it, taking medicine and having to deal with its side effects, having to mentally prepare for future situations such as a presentation, using rituals we get attached to, seeking help from a psychologist or only being able to handle certain situations under a high amount of nervousness or anxiety. When our life is based on these kinds of sacrifices, we are no longer able to be fully alive. And when the pressure becomes too much for us to handle, we try to find relief by taking drugs, becoming obsessed with power and recognition, or we fall into a depression losing motivation in life altogether.

What may actually be happening

Pressure never comes from the *outside*, even if it may seem and feel that way. This also indicates that others do not have any power over us unless we seemingly give it away to them. Yet, as long as we are other-directed, we get the impression that pressure comes from external sources such as our boss, partner, parents, friends, job, role or society. But once we become more inner-directed, we come to realize we are the only ones who can put ourselves under pressure. To illustrate this, let's take a look at a concrete example that all of us have experienced before: peer pressure.

In this context, we define peer pressure as someone only engaging in certain activities such as drinking or driving a luxury car because all other members of a particular group one desires to be part of shows the same behavior, despite him not enjoying the activity per se. If we do not engage in drinking while everyone else does, the group members try to convince us either directly or indirectly to drink, too. So, if they successfully convince us to drink despite us not wanting to, what is it that makes us drink: pressure coming from the group, us or something else? Let's have a closer look at this mechanism. The group is asking us to engage in a certain behavior and we have the choice between saying *yes* and *no*. The key factor in this decision-making process is whether we want to base our self-worth on belonging to that group or not. If our self-worth depended on that particular group of people, we would most likely pressure ourselves to say *yes* and in a way *pay a price* for belonging to the group. It is essential to note that, contrary to our assumption, there is never any pressure coming from any group. The group itself is powerless. The pressure for saying *yes* solely comes from us, which is caused by our desire to belong to the group in order to be worth something. Without this desire, it is the easiest thing in the world to say *no*. Now, we may think *But if I did not care about that particular group of people, why would I even bother spending time with them?* There is a fine but significant difference between enjoying each other's company for the joy of sharing and celebrating life and doing the same to build our self-worth or to try to impress people in order for them to like us. In the latter case, we would *prostitute* ourselves by engaging in activities for the sole purpose of getting something in return, but not doing it out of inner joy. Ironically, does this not sound familiar when we think of what we do at work and how we behave in our relationships every day? And if this is the case, is this really how we want to live life?

What we just illustrated with regard to peer pressure is also true for any kind of other pressure we face as professional athletes, business people or citizens. As soon as we use any activity to build our self-worth, we bring pressure into the system. And all of a sudden, we are no longer in it to play and do the activity in a light-hearted way, but are forced to fight, struggle and act seriously. As a consequence, it feels as if the particular job, tennis match or relationship were a matter of life and death. In life, we never have to be serious about anything. It is enough to be playful and sincere – which you can read more about under *Myth 15*.

At the same time, it is essential to understand that pressure is never caused by or inherent to situations or activities. In case we believe that certain activities themselves, such as talking in front of a big crowd, playing an important tournament or presenting ourselves in a job interview, pressure us, we may want to look again. What drains our energy is not the situations themselves, but the meaning we give and how we cope with them. All of us have experienced situations, which, at some point, used to cause pressure, but no longer stress us at all. Obviously, this is not because the activity as such has changed, but our attitude towards it. Having the latter in mind, we could also say pressure is a result of trying to fit future events to a pre-imagined stencil, hoping they will turn out the way we imagined. Having such expectations is what causes the pressure, not the situation itself. The ability to drop any expectations we may have gives us the power to create long-lasting peace in our life. The more control we believe we have over life's future events and circumstances, the more pressure we encounter because that belief itself opens up the possibility to take right or wrong decisions or actions. This way, we are seemingly under permanent pressure. For the pressure not to arise in the first place, it is enough to see how much control we actually have – which is described under *Myth 7*.

We can now go a step further and state that pressure does not even come from us. On the one hand, for most of us, it is not very hard to understand that ultimately all pressure does not come from others, but from us; and many people I have spoken to would agree with this – at least on an intellectual level. What we are capable of understanding and how we behave in everyday life, though, is usually a different thing. On the other hand, most of us do not understand the statement that it is not *us* causing the pressure either. If the pressure did not come from us, where then would it come from? The answer to this is twofold: firstly, it comes from beliefs and conditioning, which obviously are not our nature. And they can only seemingly control us, if we are not aware of their mechanism. And secondly, pressure only takes place in the world of form, but we are the formless. Although pressure may originate from the body-mind structure, it never comes from and never touches our essence; in the same way as clouds never leave a trace in the sky.

This is not about having to acquire new beliefs, but about entertaining the possibility that what you are is beyond what you usually take yourself to be through the means of thoughts and feelings. It is in no way about ignoring the pressure you may currently experience in your daily life, but about seeing it for what it actually is. The understanding of this delivers a long-lasting remedy beyond what you will ever be able to imagine.

What kind of pressure do you feel in your life? Where does that pressure originate?

Which state of mind are you in when you feel pressure? Is your attention rather on the past, the future or the now?

SPACE FOR INSPIRATION & CREATIVITY

4

You are good enough

by nature

Earn your worth by
getting to the top.

MYTH 13 – I HAVE TO EARN MY WORTH THROUGH THE APPROVAL OF OTHERS

I have never wished to cater to the crowd; for what I know they do not approve, and what they approve I do not know.
– Epicurus, born in 341

What we believe or seemingly experience to be true

All of us experience moments, in which we feel we are not good enough, although we may have one of the most recognized and highest-paying jobs, a great family and everything else society values. But no matter how successful we already may be, there is always this subtle feeling that we have to do more in order to be worthy. It is not enough to achieve just any goal, but it has to be one that certain recognized people appreciate and approve. For instance, it would not be enough to be successful in something that only our mother or our close friends appreciate. We want more than that. Only if our boss or some acknowledged leader recognizes our work, we are happy – although only for a brief moment.

Some of us may not be bothered about how high the ranks of the ones approving are, but about how *cool* or how *legendary* he or she is in a certain field we care about or want to belong to, which could be anything from a legendary *hippie* to a charismatic investment banker. Although we may claim or even feel that we do everything just to please ourselves, when looking a bit more closely, we quickly realize that almost everything we do is linked to seeking approval from others.

What may actually be happening

We are good enough by nature! No action, achievement, possession, change in appearance or anything else will ever make us worth more or less than what we already are at any given moment. It never has and it never will. Not even success, fame, certificates, titles or wins have the ability to make us a better human compared to others and compared to who we were before. For this reason, it is also okay to seemingly *fail* because it is part of a natural process within the game called life.

Yet, every day, we believe and act as if we were not worthy by just being who we are. Instead, we believe we have to achieve or produce something valuable to be worthy; or what most of us do, we think we have to belong to a certain company, club or group of people to satisfy our seeming need for belonging. If we manage to please particular people, we feel very good for a brief moment, but then very quickly, we are again in the *rat race* eager to collect our next approval by achieving a new result. And if a person or an accredited institution that means something to us tells us we are not good enough, we feel as if we failed or were not worth much. This race never seems to end. There is never a moment, which would allow us to say something such as *Now, I am finally worthy. No matter what comes next, I am worth it. I am good enough.* We make our happiness dependent on what we or other people think of us, and at the same time, wonder why we care so much about what others think of us. This is how we give away the power over our happiness to others and our own thinking.

It is rarely the case anymore, especially when it comes to our professional life, that we do things from a pure inner drive. We have forgotten how it is to *play* and be like children, that is, doing everything with ease and a sense of light-heartedness. It is not enough for us to just be who we are, express our creativity and do what comes to us from moment to moment. It seems as if life were not about being alive but about fulfilling expectations, our own and mainly the ones of others. So, the question arises whether it is possible to live a life, in which we do activities from a pure inner drive, for the joy of doing something, while at the same time being *successful*. That is, can we live a life, in which we do not need to seek approval from others and still be worth something?

As long as we believe it is possible to earn our worth, we are prone to seemingly walk on a path of constant struggle and suffering, which represents what most of us do every day. In order to be *immune* to this, it is essential to understand that who we are is beyond the concept of being worthy or not. The self-worth we idolize and chase every day is completely illusory. Yet, we carelessly give away our ease of being, which, as a consequence, is now at the mercy of arbitrary outside events and people, such as whether or not we reach a certain objective or receive a certain approval. Accordingly, we either feel amazing or sad, which no longer is in our hands. It is everything but wise to build our self-worth on ever-changing outside events we are not in control of. The key to bring about a change is to be aware of what exactly is going on. No self-help method, relaxation exercise or meditation can solve this for us; they would merely help to treat the symptoms, but would not solve the problem. While caring what other people think of us and constantly seeking approval are the symptoms, the underlying cause is the assumption that we can do something to be worthy in the first place.

For instance, I meet many people wondering why they cannot stop thinking about what others think of them. While they try to let go, they are not aware their self-worth is still based on the approval of others. So, even if they managed to forcefully stop worrying about what others think of them through some kind of method or technique, they would probably feel worse than before because their body-mind structure is still programmed to receive approval from the outside, but no longer receives it. In such case, the problem remains because they still have the assumption deep down that it is possible to gain more self-worth. It is not enough to tell people to stop caring about what other people think of them. But it is enough to see the entire mechanism behind it.

In case we notice thoughts telling us that it is part of being human to care about what other people think of us, let's challenge those, too. As opposed to our belief, when we no longer care about what others think of us, we are actually able to experience life in a much richer way. When the horses are in front of the carriage, we are finally able to notice and express our feelings fully.

Let's take a look at an example from my life, which I think is representative for what many of us experience. In my early teens, I was a very good tennis player and won almost all the matches I played on a state and national level. Without being aware back then, I enjoyed tennis not just for the fun, but also for it giving me big gains of seeming self-worth. Due to the success, people started to treat me extremely nicely and talked very highly of me. I even received small sponsorship deals with internationally recognized brands. Since I did not really understand how to deal with the entire situation, I started to believe I am a better human than others. Not only better than the other tennis players I beat, but also better than people in general. Instead of benefiting me, this attitude had actually become a big burden because I got *addicted* to recognition and held on to it so much that I was afraid of losing it. All of this, of course, I only understood years after. One of the biggest lessons in my life was during a phase, in which I unexpectedly lost many tennis matches. This made me realize people only liked me for my tennis skills, or strictly speaking, for being around someone successful, but not for who I was. Since most people stopped being so nice, the feeling of being better than others was suddenly replaced by a feeling of being worse. While before starting competitive tennis there was no judgment of being worth more or less at all, suddenly I was caught up in a world, in which there was the possibility of being either better or worse than others dependent on my performance in tennis. And only much later, I realized this is not a given reality, but something I created for myself through my attitude, and I am the only one who can put this right again. We usually assume just because our worldview or attitude changes, for instance from non-judgmental to judgmental, the world as such changes, too. But this is not the case. What changes is *only* how *we* see the world, but the change does not become an inherent attribute of the world itself. It is us who give everything all the meaning it has.

So, without being aware, my motivation to play tennis was mainly to get approval from others for how valuable and great I am. Once I no longer received the approval, due to the losses, I felt worthless and started to question everything. But as soon as I started to win matches again, I held on to the approvals of others anew. During that time, I even started to forget what it meant to have fun when playing tennis. Tennis turned into a business of receiving self-worth, and hence, became a matter of life and death. This made me experience many moments, in which I was fed up with tennis and the world. This is also the reason many athletes and business people are fed up with what they do. Jobs as such are never difficult, including all the talking, making decisions, writing and meeting people, but what is exhausting is fueling and defending our self-worth all day, every day. Even the most beautiful activity in the world becomes exhausting if we make our self-worth dependent on its outcome.

I repeated that self-worth game in my business career when I joined one of the biggest companies in the world. On surface, I felt very good working for such a company because I could hide behind its great reputation. My colleagues and I thought the higher our position in the company, the more important and better we were as a human being. Therefore, everyone in the company was eager to climb the career ladder. It was more important what other people thought of me than how I really felt inside. So, I put myself up with constant stress thinking to myself that I am stronger than most others. I acted very nicely towards certain people just to use them to my benefit to climb even higher in the ranks. This is a common and openly discussed strategy in such companies and is everything but being authentic. Over time, the lack of authenticity made me feel numb and empty inside. Although I learned very much about the art of leading businesses, building iconic brands and leading people, the sacrifice was that I did not follow my heart, intuition, and dreams, which was a very high price to pay. Deep down, I always knew that what I was doing was naïve, also because my attention was more on pleasing others than on how I felt, until one day I just quit out of the blue. And for the first time in my life, I took a big decision based on following my heart and not on pleasing others. It is one thing to know that we do not follow our intuition, and another to act accordingly. The relief was huge and everything afterwards has been an amazing journey.

Even in seemingly insignificant everyday situations such as sharing the news or gossiping about celebrities, we try to impress others by being the first ones to share something new and exciting. It builds our illusory self-worth demonstrating to others they should spend more time with us because we provide them with hot off the press information that they care about. Next time you engage in this kind of activity, be aware and observe what is happening.

Not that there is a need for labeling, but just to bring across a point, we could say there are three degrees of attachment to one's reputation, which is directly linked to how much we seek approval from others: firstly, people who care more about their reputation than anything else. This is only obvious for us if we are not caught in this mechanism as well. Especially when it comes to their profession, they are driven to impress and please others. They are neither aware of what they are caught up in nor of the harm they do to themselves, which keeps them *imprisoned* in their pattern. Paradoxically, they may even believe they are smarter than everybody else because they receive a high paycheck or lead a big team. Secondly, there are people who pretend not to care about their reputation. But when observing them from the *outside*, that is, when we are not caught in this same mechanism, we see they actually do care without them being aware. And thirdly, there are truly authentic people who sincerely do not care about their reputation, embodying this in their everyday activities. When interacting with them, we immediately recognize this, but again, only as long as we are not caught up in any of the other two degrees described above. People from those first two degrees may even judge such a person a *softie* or *stupid* because what they do may not make sense to them. At the same time, those are the people who help to make us aware of our own patterns of trying to impress others, achieving this by their sheer presence. Being around those kind of people invites us to be fully ourselves. And paradoxically, many times they are the most successful people.

On the one hand, a life based on the belief that we can earn our self-worth is as if we had invested in stocks and anxiously had to check their progress every day. How we then feel becomes dependent on outside situations such as how others behave and what others think of us. We are happy when the stocks go up and unhappy when they go down. Similarly, we are excited when someone compliments us and feel down when someone criticizes us. On the other hand, when being worthy without having to do a thing for it, we are free to follow our heart, no matter what happens with or around us. That way, things come easily because our path is in line with the natural flow of life. Such a way of living allows us to be significantly more active than ever before. Our happiness is no longer dependent on what other people think of us and on what happens in the world. When we do not invest in the stock market, its movements and changes do not have the power to affect us in any way. Similarly, when we do not invest our energy in getting approval from others, we can finally treat others as human beings and no longer as sheer instruments to achieve our selfish goals. I invite you that you do not only keep this at a theoretical level, but that you see for yourself what profound impact this can have on your life and on the people around you.

What are activities, in which the anticipated approval of others motivates you more than the activity itself?

Which activities would you continue doing even if the approval of others did no longer matter?

SPACE FOR INSPIRATION & CREATIVITY

MYTH 14 – I HAVE THE NEED TO BE LOVED

Your task is not to seek for love, but merely to seek and find all the barriers within yourself that you have built against it.
– Rumi, born in 1207

What we believe or seemingly experience to be true

We think every human has certain needs such as water, food, shelter, sexual intimacy, belonging and being loved. If we satisfy those needs on a regular basis, we are fulfilled and balanced. In our society, we attach great importance to the need for being loved. This starts at birth with the need for receiving love from our parents, later also from our friends, again later also from our boyfriend or girlfriend and at some point from our husband, wife or partner.

To make sure we receive the necessary love on a regular basis, we think it is easier to have one dedicated someone or a job providing us with this love, acceptance and respect on a more continuous, mutual basis. Therefore, we either hold on to a romantic relationship, a career or both, from which we hope to be able to satisfy our need to be loved.

Due to the belief of having to satisfy this need, we usually end up jumping into a relationship rather than finding a partner we deeply and truly resonate with, which often results in having to compromise substantially, without even being aware of it. Later on, that very compromise is the underlying cause for many conflicts between our partner and us. In our career, the situation is similar. We no longer engage in jobs to light-heartedly follow what we love or to use it as a simple source of income, but it has become something highly important we use to satisfy our need for belonging. This is also why many people feel more than just down when they are laid off or leave their jobs. Very often, the primary reason for acquiring money, driving expensive cars, becoming spiritually advanced, being vegan or having a well-reputed job is our need for belonging, acceptance and being loved and not the thing itself.

What may actually be happening

The same way the sun does not need to be shined on, what we are does not need to be loved. Yet, what we take ourselves to be is in constant need for acceptance and love, which, at the same time, is the cause for our suffering.

Generally, we act as if we were an empty bucket, whose nature is loneliness and fear. Identifying as this bucket, we believe we need to fill our lack with acceptance, respect and love, which, by the way, is also reinforced by media, advertising, corporations, parents, teachers, colleagues and friends every day. We hope to receive this love in form of a service in return by working hard in our job, creating a family, building a house, acquiring more money, going on a spiritual path, using drugs or traveling the world. Yet, the relief we get through those activities is always only of temporary nature, although we somehow hope that the next one will bring ultimate remedy. We end up hoping for the latter for the rest of our life because we never experience this ultimate remedy within the *realm* of the empty bucket.

Have you ever questioned whether you are really lonely and afraid deep down? Is this really your starting point? Or is it possible that you have accepted this idea from your surroundings without ever having validated it for yourself? Have you ever asked yourself *who* is lonely or *who* is the one that has the need to be loved? Is this really *you*? Not on a theoretical level, but by sincerely asking yourself, without looking for an answer in your head. What are you deep down? What is your essence? No book or other human will ever be able to tell you this – you can only see this for yourself.

To illustrate that there is no such thing as the need to be loved, we will look at this from three different perspectives: from the point of view of the body-mind, the energy body and our essence. While the first two perspectives belong to the world of form, the third one belongs to the formless.

First of all, we cannot solve any problems by the same means that brought them in the first place. As long as we seek remedy on the illusory body-mind level, we will always remain within this realm and encounter problems and suffer – no matter how much fame, money or success we may have. Being identified with the body-mind, we see problems when there are not any because this *fabricated* perspective itself is the cause for problems in the first place, not events or situations as such.

This may become more obvious when we understand that different people interpret one and the same event in different ways. For instance, if a boss calls several of his employees *idiots*, the ones identifying very strongly with their job might worry to such a degree that they are afraid their boss will lay them off. The ones not identified with the job, but who also perform well, are not bothered at all because his words do not trigger them to start worrying. The problem for some of these people is not derived from the situation per se, that is, the boss calling them *idiots*, but from their perspective or the meaning they give to this particular situation. Similarly, being able to overcome a situation that once used to cause suffering but now leaves us completely calm shows that we do not necessarily solve a problem by changing the situation, but by changing our attitude towards it.

The nature of the body-mind is to always seek more, no matter which goal it has already reached, how much respect and love it has already received and how many spiritual epiphanies it has already had. Among all its desires, to be loved is its ultimate one. Yet, at the same time, even being loved is not enough to get long-lasting satisfaction because nothing in this realm does. Furthermore, from the point of view of the body-mind, we are attached to the idea of having to do something or showing effort in order to be loved. But thereby, we are not able to fully appreciate the love we already receive from others because we are not open to embrace it. Instead, we are busy fighting for it, which makes all of our relationships highly mechanical. In this context, it is noteworthy that the body-mind is never the problem, but instead the identification with it, which seemingly *enslaves* us to its *insatiable* desires.

Let's see if we are able to entertain the possibility that the body does not have any needs, while at the same time agreeing with the statement that the human body intakes enough liquid and goes through other procedures every day to stay alive. In order for us not to reject this unconventional statement, it is essential to distinguish between the conceptual and the direct experience level. As long as we confuse the two, we are not even able to reflect on this, but rather label the statement as *crazy*. A need is not a fact that exists somewhere in the world out there, but is rather a fear-based state of mind that we seemingly bring into the world in form of a concept that makes any activity problematic. When looking more closely at our body from this need-based perspective, we realize that it does not only have the need to drink, eat and reproduce, but also to pump its heart, cleanse its liver, digest food, split and renew its cells and so on; the list is endless and way beyond what our mind would ever be able to grasp. If we pictured all the processes our body goes through every day to stay alive, we could get immensely worried not to be able to satisfy all of those needs. We would probably no longer be able to do anything but to worry about life. In contrast, when trusting in life and using our first-hand experience, we let the universal intelligence manage the survival of the body – which, by the way, is also the *one* taking care of everything else including making trees and plants grow, flowers bloom, our digestion work and countless other essential activities function. Through this trust, we light-heartedly drink when we are thirsty, eat when we are hungry and continuously breathe air while none of those activities demonstrate any problem. The point here is to see that a need is not a fact or something we have to think or worry about – as it is usually presented to us – but rather derives from a state of fear. The same is true for the seeming need for being loved.

Secondly, since the need for being loved is of conceptual nature, it does not exist from the perspective of the energy body. At the same time, however, we do not suggest to ignore the effect of being loved or not because it plays a significant role on an energetic level. Being able to make the discernment of which activities and people uplift us and which ones put us down has the power to change our everyday life tremendously. For instance, the belief of having the need to be loved always takes away energy. Alternatively, receiving love from another person without having any expectations gives us energy and has an uplifting or even a healing effect. Observe this in your life, during or after you meet certain people and become aware of the energy exchange. The more we understand this, the more we are able to live on high energy levels. When we are not aware of this, we seemingly remain at the mercy of other people and situations and may even end up resonating with those telling us that we have certain needs.

Thirdly, from the perspective of what we truly are, it is never possible to encounter a lack of love! What we are cannot have more or less love. To make this statement more tangible, let's take a closer look at the nature of our essence. Under what kind of circumstances does our essence reveal itself? Is it when we are busy or rather when we are in a relaxed state? Our essence freely expresses itself when we let go. And how do we feel when letting go? At rest! When being relaxed, fully present and mindful, we are aware of a deep joy, which does not have the attributes of a feeling that comes and goes, but it is the very presence, which allows us to be aware of feelings, thoughts and sounds. In this *space*, we are able to observe everything around us with great clarity. It is the state of all states, which strictly speaking, is not even a state, but our true nature. Therefore, we are not an empty bucket, but love itself – not love in form of an idea or a feeling between two people, but as the essence of what we are. It would be inappropriate to think we had to sit down thinking we are love, and then try to feel it; the latter is a common fallacy that keeps us within the realm of the empty bucket. Also, this is not to be confused with believing we have to smile and hug everyone all the time, which would illustrate we mistake the form for the formless – the latter being a common phenomenon that can be found in certain spirituality, yoga or mindfulness circles. Since we can never become what we already are, it is rather much different. When letting go of everything, what remains is a deep sense of what we are, which could be described as joy, peace or love. Even the body-mind construct in its essence is made of the formless, and hence, the form can never become or even grasp the formless. Once we see the false for the false, we will be aware of what we already are, and we realize there is not even the need to let go. When trying to put truth into words, or rather pointing towards it, it always sounds a bit *foolish* to our rational mind. So, instead of believing what you are reading here, feel and see it for yourself.

Who are the people in your life that you try to please?

How do you feel in the very moment you try to please others?

SPACE FOR INSPIRATION & CREATIVITY

5

The outside is a reflection of your inside

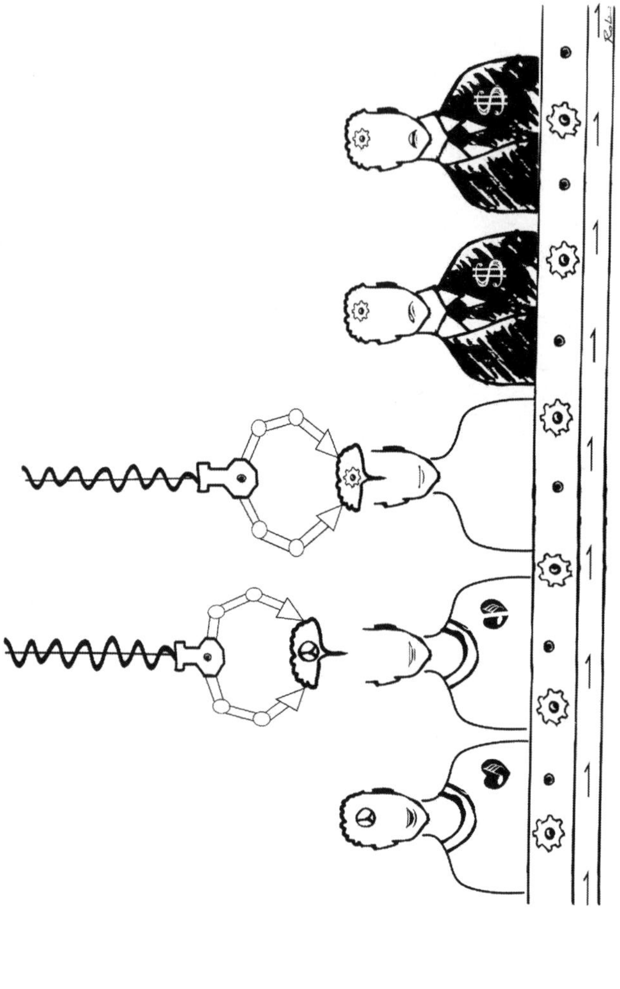

MYTH 15 – I HAVE TO BE SERIOUS IN LIFE

Dance, when you're broken open. Dance, if you've torn the bandage off. Dance in the middle of the fighting. Dance in your blood. Dance when you're perfectly free.
– Rumi, born in 1207

What we believe or seemingly experience to be true

The older we get, the more serious life seems to become. In contrast, almost everything children engage in is playful. During childhood we are still *immune* to our parents and other adults trying to convince us of taking things seriously, and we also do not yet have the belief that we are obliged to do certain things. But sooner or later, usually during our teens, we slowly start to become more serious in life. Amongst others, we are conditioned that way through repetitive messages such as *One day, you have to get a job, otherwise you may end up on the street* or *You cannot just sit around and dream all day or You have to be disciplined and work hard in life*.

Overall, we tend to segment life into two parts: on the one hand, there is the serious part, which includes working, creating a family, building a house, organizing one's life, and fighting for one's reputation; and on the other hand, there is the fun part, which includes activities such as going to parties, drinking alcohol, going on a vacation or hanging out with friends. While it is socially accepted to be playful in our free time, we are expected to be rather serious when it comes to work and other responsibilities.

The more serious we are, the more weight lies on our shoulders, the more greedy we are, the less we smile, the less we help others, the more we try to find short-term relief and the more we see life as if it were a constant fight against others and especially against ourselves.

What may actually be happening

Nothing in life is serious. Life as such is playful through and through. Yet, it appears to us as if it were inherently serious due to us acquiring seriousness through our upbringing, and even more so by identifying with phenomena every day, although the latter not having anything to do with who we are – not even in the slightest way.

Let's take a closer look at what it actually means to be serious. When being in a serious state of mind, something deep down does not feel right to us. This becomes obvious, for instance, when someone does an impression of us of how serious we are at a particular moment. While that provocative, yet playful indication may agitate us, we intuitively know we are not ourselves when being serious. Seriousness is a state of mind characterized by other-directedness, which is derived from a feeling of having to meet certain expectations coming from outside. It is a fearful, narrow-minded, contracted state, in which we hope the future will or won't turn out in a certain way. When being serious, we try to escape fear by pretending to be focused, disciplined and responsible. Paradoxically, nobody, except for children and people who are not stuck in this pattern, notices anything strange when we are serious because it is a socially accepted behavior. All of us have had moments, in which we told our friends or family members not to distract us because we are busy engaging in something serious such as work. When such moments occur more frequently, we intuitively know something does not feel right, realize we are not happy and would actually prefer to be more relaxed and able to smile or laugh with the people around us. The more we become aware of this mechanism, the more *foolish* we feel for pretending to be so serious. Furthermore, we act as if being serious were a prerequisite for becoming successful. At some point in our upbringing we start to confuse becoming successful with being serious, which is partly brought about by parents, politicians and successful people on television, who appear to be extremely serious. Examples for typical thought patterns coming from a serious state of mind are *This time, I cannot mess this up, so I better make it happen*, or *I just have to be disciplined enough to show others I am capable of doing this job*, or *I cannot mess this up because this child depends on me to survive*, or *I cannot just sit around and enjoy life, I also need to show others that I am worth it* or *If I do this job properly, I will get that promotion and then finally, I can relax*.

Seriousness is strongly linked to reputation, that is, our constant struggle for defending an image we have about ourselves towards others. As soon as someone says something about us, which is not in line with our image, we get threatened, and hence, become very serious and fearful. Due to our immense obsession with our reputation, others do not even necessarily have to say anything, but it is already enough to trigger our seriousness by just thinking what others may think of us when we behave in a certain way or do certain activities. We have acquired the belief that what we are needs to have a very good reputation to make an impression on others. And since we know that one wrong behavior on our side can destroy our reputation, we are constantly obsessed with fueling and defending our image, which keeps us in a wheel of seriousness.

Taking things personally also causes high amounts of seriousness. We often hear we should not take things so personally, but do not really know what this actually means. It means we worry about our reputation and about what others think of us in an obsessive way without even being aware of it. It is the belief that everything in life is not just happening, but is happening *to us*. As a result, everything in life becomes personal, which makes us prone to get hurt and fearful. All of us intuitively know that taking something personally or seriously is not good for us, but we continue to do so because we are not aware of this mechanism in our everyday life, and hence, we believe life is serious by nature.

So, what exactly happens between childhood and adulthood, that is, what makes us become so serious in the first place? From the point of view of a child, being playful dominates everything we do. We do not bother with whom we play, how long we play and whether we will ever play again with a certain child. We may cry for a moment, but then move on to the next moment as if nothing ever happened. We are not really concerned about what will happen tomorrow or what will happen next week. If we were as serious and concerned during childhood as we are as adults, we would constantly worry about life because so many things could and will go *wrong* along the way. Nevertheless, we are not bothered at all because we take everything in a light-hearted and playful way. Yet, at some point, the conditioning or *brainwashing* with regard to becoming serious kicks in, which is a slow but certain process that lasts for years and goes as follows: first of all, we are completely *immune* and have no understanding of what adults try to tell us. Then, we strongly resist, and finally, we give in. It works so effectively because we receive the same message from different sources, such as teachers, parents, students and media. Once *brainwashed*, we not only believe this new *reality* to be true, but even start our own propaganda for it; firstly, convincing ourselves, later our peers and at some point even our own children. One of the most essential differences between our way of living as children and adults is that as children we do not yet have the belief that we could be doing something different from what we are doing right now. If we were able to see that this very belief takes away our playfulness, we would be able to be content no matter where and with whom we are at any given moment. Seeing this is essential in making our life more light-hearted. This very belief is what brings seriousness and worries into our life, never activities as such, whether it is washing the dishes or any other activity we may not enjoy.

Being serious does not only not feel good, but can also hinder us from being successful. During my teens, I was a very good tennis player and partly expected to win because I felt I was one of the most serious players. I constantly analyzed other players and worried about whether I could beat them or not. When I saw other players who were rather light-hearted and won more matches than me or even beat me, I could never understand how they managed to be better without being serious at all. Somehow, I mistakenly believed there is a positive correlation between taking something seriously and being successful. Now, I can clearly see how being serious rather hinders us from being more successful. Seriousness springs from fear, but to be successful on the tennis court, it is essential to be deeply relaxed on the inside. Therefore, there is never a moment, in which we need to be serious. It is enough to be sincere, which means to be authentic, truthful and responsible without any vibrations of fear attached.

So, the question arises whether it is at all possible to transpose the playfulness we experienced during childhood into our routine as adults? The first step in doing so is to become fully aware that we seemingly have a veil made of basic seriousness around us that makes us anxious every day. Bringing playfulness into our life does not only mean to carry out more playful activities such as playing board games, playing ball in the park or telling each other jokes, but it mainly means to do whatever we are engaged in in a playful and sincere way at any given moment. For instance, instead of washing dishes with the mindset of *I hate doing the dishes*, we do it in a playful way, enjoy the contact with water and see it as something we are grateful for; but grateful not for doing the activity itself, but for being present. To take true effect, it is essential the playfulness is not happening only on a thought level, but it is authentically sensed in the body – else, it remains a purely irrelevant and theoretical exercise. The second step in bringing more playfulness into our life is to essentially understand that life inherently is neither serious nor not serious because we give everything all the meaning it has. Only when truly understanding this, we are able to bring about a change. Else, we may just be banging our head against a brick wall without even noticing it. Take a moment and look at this in your own life right now. Is life serious or are you making it so? I invite you not to look for the answer on a thought level.

I know someone whose life had been completely transformed through the power of playfulness. He used to strongly suffer from fear and panic attacks, and for years, he tried countless conventional and unconventional methods to deal with it including modern and ancient medicine, psychotherapy, meditation, spirituality, shamanic medicine, yoga, and so on. But nothing had really worked for him. The turning point was when he spontaneously picked up a ball. Instead of meeting his friend for a coffee as usual, they went to the park to play ball. Through that simple yet playful activity, it *clicked* for him and he managed to take playfulness back into his everyday life getting rid of the depression. In that very moment, he realized he was depressed because he forgot that life is not serious, but rather a play. Obviously, the point here is not to suggest that picking up a ball will bring ultimate remedy for everyone, but to understand on a deeper level that authentic playfulness can be the remedy for many illnesses and the solution for some of us may lie in rediscovering this playfulness. What we can say for certain is that there is a strong link between being playful and living a light-hearted life.

Taking a step back, we may come to realize that we are in this world to play, dance and express ourselves, and not to be serious, struggle for or fight against anything. When looking at life from this wider perspective, we may be able to entertain that even the seriousness and the struggle is part of the play. The problem with seriousness is not necessarily seriousness per se, but the identification with it without being aware of it. That way, we are driven by fear and do not freely express who we are. One of the most beautiful moments is to turn situations, in which we used to act with seriousness into moments we are able to enjoy playfully. This helps us to see that life as such is not made of fear, but of joy. And therefore, we are not a victim of some random outside circumstances, but always have the power to change the way we experience life, and hence, how we perceive reality. And if seriousness and fear appear, we are aware that even those are part of a play called life. This way, life is no longer only about celebrating specific events, but even about celebrating life itself as a whole, which allows us to feel the joy of being alive.

In what ways has *being serious* served you?

In which situations are you rather serious? How would those situations change if you were sincere or playful instead?

SPACE FOR INSPIRATION & CREATIVITY

MYTH 16 – I NEED TO AVOID FAILURE

The price of inaction is far greater than
the cost of making a mistake.
– Meister Eckhart, born in 1260

What we believe or seemingly experience to be true

We fear mistakes and failure because we are afraid of potentially being rejected. When hearing about someone failing, we are scared we may end up being labeled a failure one day, too. Thus, we try to avoid failure to such as degree that we sometimes do not even engage in certain activities.

When making mistakes, we try everything possible to hide them, so nobody notices them, which is important to us for keeping a good reputation. If someone still found out about a mistake despite our efforts to sweep it under the rug, we would come up with sophisticated excuses to show that it was not our fault. Furthermore, we try everything in our power to downplay the mistake hoping the word does not spread, and hence, it does not hurt our reputation or career. When making mistakes, we feel embarrassed because we have the impression we are expected to be successful and not a failure in life. This is also why it is not a coincidence the word *loser* is a cussword in society.

Only when people have *succeeded* in life according to societal standards, by, for example, having set up a successful business or reaching fame, certain brave people dare to speak about failure – but otherwise it is a taboo to openly speak about it in mainstream society.

What may actually be happening

By nature, nobody has ever made any mistakes or failed because it is simply not possible to do so. We can only seemingly fail when we engage in activities for the sole purpose of reaching a certain goal. In such case, we do not truly enjoy the activity, but mainly care about its outcome. Hypothetically assuming failure did exist, it could be defined as *to engage in activities we do not enjoy – independent of whether the outcome is good or not*. Alternatively, when we fully enjoy a certain activity, it is impossible to fail because we experience joy during the activity itself and not through its outcome. Since these statements are far from what we believe to be true or hear every day, let's shed some light on this.

We call something a mistake or failure when a certain activity does not correspond with the image we, others or society have of that activity or its outcome; or put differently, we believe we fail when we do not meet certain expectations. Mistakes and failure do not have an existence on their own, but only seemingly exist in the realm of thoughts, or more specifically only related to preconceived, conceptual expectations. For example, when throwing a ball towards a basket, we can only seemingly fail when we are attached to the conceptual expectation of the ball having to go into the basket. Without having an image or expectation of how something should look like, it is not possible to make any mistakes or fail. However, for most of us, mistakes appear to be real and cause suffering because we are obsessed with or even hypnotized by thoughts. We have been conditioned in a way that we are seemingly no longer in touch with what is beyond thinking, that is, the now, which is not a moment in time.

In this context, it is essential to understand that the problem is not the belief in the concept of failure per se, but our self-worth being attached to it, which makes all the difference. Even if we believed in failure, it would never be able to touch us as long as we do not link the result of an activity to how worthy we are. But as soon as we build our self-worth, for instance, on throwing a ball into a basket, failure becomes a problem because it is no longer just about a ball going into a basket, but about whether or not we are worth something before others and ourselves dependent on the outcome of where the ball goes. Therefore, mistakes and failure are never inherent to situations or to life, but it is rather that we seemingly bring them into reality. This is not an attempt to escape or think positively, but to invite you to go beyond the realm of thinking.

There is much confusion about how to appropriately manage expectations with regard to unleashing one's full potential in the world of sports and high performance overall. What usually happens is the following: athletes intuitively know that putting their attention on expectations does not help them to stay calm and perform at their best, and hence, they tell themselves not to have any. However, they are not aware that expectations not only take effect on the mental plane, but also deeply impact their entire body, coordination and energy systems. Consequently, their attempt to *think* not to have expectations only addresses the realm of thinking, which obviously is not enough to show efficacy overall because the deep conditioning of their physical and energy body still takes strong effect on them. Therefore, trying to let go of expectations on the thinking level may even weaken them overall because their energy and body systems still hold on to expectations, which means the overall system is not sure in which direction to move, which causes confusion on all levels. Doing so would be similar to someone not knowing how to swim, but still going into deep waters assuming it would be enough to *think* he knows how to swim without realizing that the body and energy system is what is key in holding the body over water. Although it seems most obvious, what is described here is what the vast majority of people and athletes try to do, not knowing how to practice their body and mind holistically. Based on my coaching experience with athletes and business people, the majority of them do not embody this, even if many of them have already reflected on this for many years. They are stuck because they do not see beyond the realm of thinking, which by the way is easily accessible to each one of us.

Let's further illustrate the illusion of failure by looking at a few examples. The first time we are formally confronted with the matter of failure is when taking tests in school. At a young age, most of us study for exams because we try to avoid failing and please our parents with good grades, as opposed to being intrinsically motivated to learn. If it were up to us, instead of going to school we would rather play with other children. Yet, being stuck in school, we do not really challenge the concept of failing, but rather learn to blindly accept it as part of a seeming reality that others created for us. We see what negative consequences, reactions and emotions are triggered in others when they fail, which is also the reason we try to avoid it altogether. The concept of failure is used to condition us to do certain activities we would not engage in if we were free to follow our inner drive. Those activities include studying for subjects we are not interested in and learning in a school context dominated by power, competition and fear rather than compassion and joy. This form of extrinsic motivation does not only work well in school, but also in the working world. So-called experts claim that around 70 to 80 percent of people are not motivated at work. When looking at those numbers and at the people around us, it almost seems as if their objective in life were to engage in activities they do not enjoy, be around people they do not like and be afraid of failing at that. This fear-based, extrinsic motivation model is so effective in manipulating us because we are already conditioned in school to believe we are better humans when we have better grades than others. And later in the working world, grades are replaced by how much we earn, how high our rank is and how many awards we win.

When somebody gets fired from his or her job, he or she usually suffers from not feeling worthy. The lack of self-worth is not caused by someone *losing* his or her job, but by believing one failed. If our values are derived from society, we do not have a choice but to think we failed because we are *brainwashed* to believe we are in this world to have a proper job and do things we do not enjoy. In such case, not having a job makes us believe we are not good enough or something is wrong with us. Even our language reflects this belief system. Who said we could *lose* a job? It may be rather the case that we *win* freedom from doing something we never really liked in the first place. What actually happens is that we no longer engage in a certain job, which is neither good nor bad per se. But it is the meaning we give to it. The belief of having to have a job in order to be worthy is so strong that we are even afraid to quit a job on our own initiative. Alternatively, when we navigate through life listening to our intuition, we are able to confront what is happening at any given moment without feeling guilty, even in case something happens that is not valued by society.

Michael Jordan, one of the most successful basketball players in history, knew how to play basketball beyond the concept of failure. He once said something along those lines that he had *failed* over and over again, probably more than everyone else, which was the reason he succeeded. He was not scared to take the game-deciding and tough shots during crunch time. When he says he *failed* more than everyone else, it obviously shows he does not take the concept of failure seriously. Other players did not dare to take as many risky shots because they were afraid to miss. Through our upbringing, we are conditioned to rather not engage in risky activities, in which we are likely to fail in order to protect our reputation, although our intuition may encourage us to do so. For instance, this is also true for having the desire to quit a high-paid job to become an artist, but not daring to go ahead because we are afraid of failure despite us feeling numb and empty in our current job. We prioritize meeting the expectations of others and what they think of us over how *we* feel. Such a behavior springs from the fear of being labeled a failure. Since we are trained not to hang out with so-called *losers*, we do not want to become an outcast ourselves.

Often times, the fear of being labeled a failure is the reason for many children to stop their hobby. For instance, I gave many children tennis lessons in different parts of the world and what they all love is running around and having fun. But as soon as they are able to hit a few balls over the net, they start playing for points because they are prepared and conditioned to become successful tennis players one day by their coach and parents. The underlying assumption behind this is that tennis players will only become *successful* if they are able to become a very good tournament player – although for most of them success could also mean to just enjoy hitting balls. So, all children as of a certain age practice in a way as if they had the prerequisite to become a professional tennis player. However, playing points is only enjoyed by the few who beat the others. Most other players become very insecure and start hating tennis because they do not like to *lose.* Thus, most young players get the impression that tennis is all about winning because winning gets rewarded and when they lose they start feeling inferior – not just as a player, but also as a person. Even many of the highly talented players develop subtle shock reactions in certain strokes because they are afraid of missing the ball deep down to their cells. Instead of being something fun to do, tennis then becomes a serious business that mainly seems to be a matter of life and death, especially when playing on a tournament level.

It is not easy for children to still have fun that way. Most coaches use a one-size-fits-all *military style* because that is what they learned themselves. While this may help a few of the talented players to become somewhat successful, the pressure makes most others drop out at the age of around 15 or 16. Our society is no longer only competitive when it comes to school and business, but it has reached most aspects of our life. At the same time, it is essential to see that the competiveness as such is not the problem here, but when competiveness becomes a prominent attitude in our life, then it is.

Another example illustrating how the concept of failure hinders us from growing is the way we learn to walk. When learning to walk as a child, a major part of the process is to fall down. When we see our child fall down, we would never conclude that our child *failed* just because she is not able to walk the first few times she tries it. We know *failing* is part of the process of becoming stronger and acquiring new skills. The more we *fail*, the better we get at something. We would never learn to walk if we gave up after the first few attempts just because we were too afraid of being judged by our parents or others. If there were such a thing as failure, would it not be more of a failure to be enslaved to a *sick* society and be afraid of what others think than to take some risk in life to follow our dreams? Think about it.

When looking at failure in the context of business, some bigger organizations are slowly starting to understand that *failure*, or rather the method of trial and error, is part of the natural process when it comes to creating new skills, processes, innovation and successful product launches. Most of the established companies would informally admit that they have problems with delivering enough breakthrough innovations. This is partly due to their culture, which is still strongly characterized by rewarding success and avoiding or even punishing failure. Despite being extremely rich with regard to financial and human resources, big corporations struggle immensely with launching breakthrough innovations, while many startups with relatively low resources manage to launch breakthrough innovations again and again. The mindset, behavior and affinity to take risk shaped by the company culture plays a key role in this. While people in bigger and established corporations care more about their reputation to further climb the career ladder, and hence, try to avoid failure, people in startups are more likely to use their intuition, which is a great *ingredient* to have when challenging the status quo with regard to product innovations.

One of the most direct ways in making living beyond the idea of mistakes and failure a reality to is to let go of all expectations. Yes, all expectations! If you are noticing thoughts such as *But it is important to have expectations,* then look again. For me, letting go of expectations was something that happened suddenly, without me planning for it. Many years ago, I was stopping the car at a red light when it *hit* me. Just seconds before, I was very disappointed about a friend again canceling an appointment, although I was so looking forward to seeing her. In the next moment, it *clicked* and I had the deep and penetrating insight that the one and only reason I was disappointed was not my friend, but that I had the expectation that my friend should make it more of a priority in her life to see me. In that very moment, the disappointment changed into a deep feeling of joy and peace – as if the joy of an immense wisdom had been downloaded into my system. Ever since, my life has become several *tons* lighter with regard to the way I live. Having expectations means demanding the future to turn out the way we imagine it to, not being aware that we do not have any control over what will happen in the future whatsoever. Having expectations is one of the biggest causes for disappointment. They are the reason we believe failure and mistakes are possible in the first place.

Becoming aware of the underlying mechanism of the concept of mistakes and failure in the very moment they occur allows us to be free from them. A life currently characterized by fear is transformed into one of trust. This way, expectations and preconceived notions of an imaginary perfect world drop and life turns out to be perfect in its own way – which is more enriching than we could have ever dreamed of. This shifts our motivation from extrinsic to intrinsic and sets free our original and creative energy to express ourselves in our most authentic form without being afraid of being judged. Our expression is no longer driven by egocentric goals, but is finally in resonance with the sublime flow of life. That way, we are more active and playful than ever before.

What are certain activities you desire to engage in, but demonstrate inaction because you are afraid of failing at them?

When being afraid of failure, what exactly do you fear?

SPACE FOR INSPIRATION & CREATIVITY

MYTH 17 – I IMPROVE THROUGH FEEDBACK

One cannot reflect in streaming water. Only those who know internal peace can give it to others.
– Lao Tzu, born in the 6th century BC

What we believe or seemingly experience to be true

Today, the concept of feedback is widely used in organizations, especially in bigger ones. Whether in annual reviews with one's manager, after a workshop or after important meetings, managers and employees give each other feedback very frequently in either oral or written form. And even apart from work, the feedback culture plays a prominent role, which we can observe in the innumerous product and service reviews, which we use as part of our decision-making when buying something or going to a restaurant.

We consider feedback to be useful and fair because we believe it helps us to understand how we are perceived by others and improve our performance in the future. In certain organizations, feedback is even *sold* under the concept of coaching, which gives us the impression that it not only improves certain skills, but also helps us to grow personally. Additionally, being able to provide feedback about our managers makes us feel safe because it gives us the option to stand up against them just in case they do not treat us properly. Nevertheless, most of us feel uncomfortable or tense in feedback situations due to our very strong defense mechanisms and resistance that are triggered in such intense moments.

A trend that has already been going on for a few decades and is still going strong in companies is to use feedback from potential clients in connection with product launches. Managers assume that designing products based on the opinions of potential clients helps to minimize the risk of *failure*.

What may actually be happening

When feedback plays an important role in an organization, its people predominantly act out of an underlying fear of making mistakes and never feel good enough. Feedback mainly serves as a tool to make people work hard and to control them. As a result, the workforce is submissive and watches each other for not breaking the rules and principles. Even feedback outside of work very often has a low-spirited touch, which we can notice by the way it makes us feel. Being under the influence of an almost constant stream of feedback gives us the impression that it is not okay the way we are, and hence, we feel we constantly have to improve. It makes us adapt to the world instead of letting the world adapt to us. And adapting to the world never feels good because we become other-directed. Since these introductory statements may rattle our current belief system, let's take a closer look at feedback and the role it plays in our everyday life.

Feedback is based on the assumption that we have the ability to improve our future performance based on how we performed in the past. Have you ever paused for a moment asking yourself whether this is valid in the first place? Does it work for you? Why or why not? If it were true that we are able to improve the future by learning from the past, would humanity not live in *paradise* by now, after being around for millions of years and fighting innumerable wars? Did we learn anything from those wars? Haven't there been enough opportunities for us to learn from the past or through feedback from others? Or, moving our attention from the world to a specific company, if feedback really worked, would not every company be able to create a highly productive culture and launch successful breakthrough innovations every year? For instance, a leader of an organization could just ask some of the most successful employees to give everyone else ongoing feedback about how to do everything right. Or let's take a look at our personal life. If feedback really worked, would it not be the easiest thing to become amazing at everything we do? Why is it that most of the time, it does not work? Where is the catch? Is it that we struggle to implement feedback or do we simply not understand it? Or is it due to something completely different?

One of the key reasons feedback does not work the way we claim it would is that no situation in life ever repeats itself. Every moment is anew, different and so complex no mind will ever be able to comprehend. It seems the only constant in the world of form is change. But somehow we still act as if life were fully predictable assuming it consists of many constants. Using feedback to improve something would be as if we took water out of a river using a cup and then claiming we captured the essence of the river. Based on the water sample, we would seriously discuss how we could improve the river ignoring the obvious point that the river is so much more than what we are able to capture in form of a water sample. The main quality of the river is not water, but *rivering.* Additionally, feedback does not work because it is based on the invalidated assumption that we have the choice to freely think and do whatever we desire. In other words, it assumes we have free will, which is explored further under *Myth 7*.

Attempting to implement feedback from others may not only not help us to improve, but may even restrict us in certain cases. While we may manage to improve one or two isolated aspects taken out of context, it may make the situation overall worse because we ignore other, more important factors. For instance, the most inspirational speakers usually show a highly strong stage presence or charisma. If now, such a speaker was told to improve her eye contact and the structure of the presentation, she might be able to improve those particular aspects, but by focusing on improving them, she would show a significantly weaker stage presence, and hence, would no longer connect with the audience as she did before. As a result, her speech would come across as rather mechanical without the *magic* people fell in love with in the first place. Another example is from my early teens when I was ahead of other tennis players with regard to technique, stroke options and coordination. Despite my competitive advantage on those tennis-specific aspects, at some point, I started to have problems in the beginning of many of my tennis matches. The feedback I received from my parents and highly recognized coaches was that my footwork was poor, and hence, I needed to practice it to be able to run faster, which, at first, sounds as if this were a very logical thing to do. However, somehow I knew I was very good at running, which I demonstrated at practice and also once I found into the match. Not being aware of the bigger picture, I still implemented the feedback and practiced my footwork immensely, but without making any significant overall improvement. Nobody saw that the reason for my poor footwork during the beginning of tournament matches was not the poor footwork, but nervousness. Once I understood that clearly for myself, I could start to deal with the cause. But I could have never solved this if I listened to the feedback of others, including the one from so-called experts. The point here is that most of the times, feedback is given without truly understanding the cause of the problem. This is a very common course of action and does not contribute to making us better. Most of us are not really able to help others to improve, and instead just try to teach them what is valued in a certain context or what we know, without seeing what a particular situation may actually require. We usually do not know better and act mostly from preconceived notions. Put differently, being occupied with implementing isolated feedback reduces our presence, which is where the *magic* happens.

As opposed to our conventional logic, feedback and reviews are never about the person or organization receiving but about the one providing them. Why is that? For instance, let's imagine a concert, a book, a hotel stay or an inspirational speech. If 100 people from an audience were asked to provide feedback about a particular event, there would be 100 different versions of feedback. Some people may love what others hate and again some others may be inspired by what others get bored. This alone demonstrates that their feedback cannot be about the performing act, but about each one of them expressing their own interpretation of a seemingly objective outside event. This fallacy of believing feedback is about the one receiving it is closely linked to three substantial elements we already explored in this book: firstly, there are no events taking place separate from us; secondly, we are not in the world, but the world is in us; and thirdly, the observer has the biggest influence on any given experiment or event. When exploring those three statements and experiencing them first hand, we will see that feedback the way we use it is redundant because it is based on the illusion that we live in an objective world separate from us.

When an artist attempts to create a piece of art using feedback, which she may do to reach commercial success, she is not able to achieve anything of authentic and original nature. In such circumstances, she would assume she has to please as many people as possible with her work to be successful. In theory, this should leave her with a piece of art that appeals to many people. However, in practice, we all know that such a piece of art would no longer be *alive* and neither the audience nor the artist would feel connected to it because it lacks authentic expression and originality, which makes people connect with art in the first place.

A true piece of art always has the power to take us from its expression in form to our formless truth, the latter being our true nature, which is common to all of us. By demonstrating an immense presence and depth, the artist herself experiences this formless truth at the very moment of the inception of the creation and is able to magically create a snapshot of the formless in the realm of form. When marveling at the piece of art, sparks of the formless truth jump over to the open-minded beholder, which allows him to experience the same formless beauty the artist experienced at its inception.

What we observe in the world of art is also applicable to life in general. Through the feedback culture, athletics, business and many other fields are becoming more and more standardized on various levels. When doing something mechanically to just reach a materialistic goal, the use of feedback may help us to reach an average result, but not more. While it may be useful to produce short-term mainstream commercial success behind heavy investments, it hinders people from being authentic. We believe fast success comes from the commonly used *share and reapply* approach, which means we look at best-in-class cases and try to copy those as a mean to reach our egocentric goals. We try to reproduce what meets our eyes. However, again and again we are not able to succeed because we do not realize that the formless originality, which is *the* success factor that made the person or company we look up to successful in the first place, is not reproducible – but instead lies within our own originality. Paradoxically, being true and authentic not only makes us more successful within and beyond societal standards, but it also feels holistically right to us.

With regard to using feedback for launching product innovations, Henry Ford, founder of the Ford Motor Company, once said something along those lines of if he had asked his clients what they desired, they would have told him faster horses and not an engine-driven vehicle. Since feedback is limited to knowledge from the past, it does not allow us to create breakthrough innovations for the future. Despite this, many companies, especially bigger ones, still use feedback from clients in an almost religious manner spending a fortune because most of the managers have lost the ability to think for themselves and connect with their own originality within themselves, that is, the ultimate source of innovation.

The main point here is not to state that feedback is redundant per se, but to point out the impact it can have on how we feel and behave individually and as a group, if allowing it to affect us. Understanding this will help us to create relationships, company cultures and innovation processes based on trust and compassion rather than on fear. People and cultures that are connected with their own originality and are motivated intrinsically are among the happiest and most successful ones. So, instead of rigorously fitting people around a preconceived company or innovation culture, we let the originality from within the people unfold as if they played a *symphony* directed by the universal life force.

Understanding the mechanism of feedback may even help us to take it less personally. Usually, we are fully identified with it because we think it is about us. The hurtful part is never the feedback itself, but only us identifying with judgments, resistance, feelings and thoughts. It makes our life easier when we clearly see that feedback is never about us, that is the formless, but always about the form. And going a step further, the power over everything is always with us because we are the one interpreting every feedback situation giving everything all the meaning it has.

What gives you the right to tell others how to do things when providing feedback? Elaborate on your answer.

How do you feel when receiving feedback, independent of whether the feedback is positive, negative or neutral?

SPACE FOR INSPIRATION & CREATIVITY

MYTH 18 – THE HIGHEST GOAL OF ALL IS TO BE A GOOD, RESPECTED AND SUCCESSFUL CITIZEN

Be kind, for everyone you meet is fighting a hard battle.
– Plato, born in 427 BC

What we believe or seemingly experience to be true

Starting at an early age, we come to believe that life is all about adapting, trying to belong to and making our way in society. We learn how to properly behave in public, follow given moral codes, meet obligations and try to become successful and happy within society. Sooner or later, though, many of us become aware that our life goes in circles and that we keep ourselves constantly busy with issues that are not even relevant. Somehow we know there must be more to life than the ordinary.

A substantial part of our social conditioning comes from our parents and society. Without being aware, and hence, not being able to question certain essential aspects, this conditioning is passed on from generation to generation and we, in turn, raise our children based on what we absorbed from our environment. Our lack of challenging the status quo is also part of this heavy conditioning. In a way, what we teach our children is more than just social conditioning because it feels to them as if it represented a reality set in stone. Believing we are able to move around freely, think and do what we like and live a more or less happy life is proof enough to us that we are free people living in a free society.

What may actually be happening

This chapter is inspired by the well-known *Allegory of the Cave*, which Greek philosopher Plato presented about 2,400 years ago. For the purpose of grasping the key points of this chapter, you find a brief summary of the allegory in the following paragraphs, whose objective, by the way, is not to be strictly exact or exhaustive. While it is not necessary for the understanding of this chapter, I still invite you to read the full version of the allegory or watch a short video clip explaining it in more detail. Another tool that may help you to better understand the depths of the allegory is the cover illustration of this book, which is a graphic interpretation of the allegory.

Imagine a cave with prisoners sitting on the ground facing the wall at the far end of the entrance. Their feet, hands and heads are chained to the ground in a way that they are not able to turn their heads, and hence, have not seen anything but the wall in front of them since early childhood. Behind them is a fire, and between the fire and the prisoners is a walkway with people carrying certain objects that are of high significance to them. Since the prisoners never get to see the actual objects, they mistake their moving reflections and shadows projected onto the wall in front of them for their reality.

One day, one of the prisoners is freed. When he turns towards the fire on the other side, the direct, bright light starts to hurt his eyes because they had been accustomed to a world of darkness and shadows. At first, he denies what he sees and stays true to his current perception of reality thinking that the actual objects he is seeing for the first time were illusionary and the reflections he used to look at were real. But after being exposed to this new reality for a longer time, he slowly but surely comes to realize that until now he had lived a lie and eventually agrees that these actual objects are *closer to reality* than their shadows. One day, when completely being dragged out of the cave and seeing the vast variety of nature for the very first time, he again needs to adjust his eyesight to the even brighter sunlight and reorient himself towards this new realm of reality. The more time he spends under the sunlight, the more he is able to see the even bigger picture of reality and is finally able to enjoy his true freedom in the light.

Only after having experienced true freedom himself, he is able to see the actual degree of restriction and narrow-mindedness that characterizes life in the cave. He now feels compassion for his former friends and colleagues who suffer every day without even being aware of it. When returning to the cave telling his friends about the bigger picture of the reality that he experienced, he notices that they think he became *crazy* and that they defend and continue to hold on to their current mind-constructed reality, which is all they know. If asked whether they wanted to leave the cave, they would choose not to because they are afraid to become *crazy* themselves and eventually be excluded from society.

In the allegory, the cave represents society, the prisoners the people within society and the people carrying the objects the opinion makers. The allegory is highly provocative in the way that it states that *we*, the people, are in a state of ignorance, but at the same time act as if we knew reality. Translated into our everyday life, what kind of ignorance is Plato referring to when stating this? He is referring to an ignorance that usually finds expression through behavior and activities such as comparing, judging, gossiping, trying to be better than others, acquiring and holding on to degrees, titles and certificates, claiming to know everything better, trying to win debates and arguments, resisting, hiding fears, climbing on the career ladder, claiming to know the truth, striving to become something, being proud, executing power over others, maintaining one's reputation and looking for approval from others. All of those activities have in common that they seemingly separate us from others and the world and keep us running in the hamster wheel. Being ignorant, we act as if we were extremely important and constantly engaged in serious matters without being aware that instead we are lost in narrow-minded, little fights, which all take place far away from truth. Our life is a constant struggle for approval from the other people in the cave with regard to our behavior and performance. By being fully engaged in matters that are highly valued by society, we have seemingly lost our interest in truth. We live a life, in which we give more importance to being respected by society than exploring our truth beyond the vastly *sick* societal conditioning. We got into this in the first place because we are passive observers and inheritors of the opinions given to us. No theoretical knowledge or activities from within the realm of ignorance will ever help us to get out of the cave, that is, bring us closer to truth. Knowledge in our society means being able to name things, that is, dealing with the shadows of objects. And the only thing we value more than naming objects is having certificates about our ability to name objects. A first step in moving away from mistaking the shadows on the wall for reality is to follow our intuition, which tells us that there is more to life than just going to school, getting a job, building a house, raising a family and after death being remembered as a good citizen.

Despite being a prisoner in the cave, we claim we are happy because we have forgotten what it *really feels* to be free and alive outside of the cave. Instead, we create an idea about happiness in our head and rationally come to the conclusion whether or not we are happy. In this context, some of us claim to be happy although we work between 35 and 70 hours every week. When we work like a *modern slave* but claim to be happy, we answer from a pure idea level, comparing ourselves with people who may have a less valued job, earn less or work harder. This would be similar to a whale being caught in a zoo for many years and when assessing its current state of happiness or freedom, it would compare it to how it felt on other days in the zoo, having almost completely forgotten about how it is to live in true freedom in the ocean.

Ultimately, our attention follows where our desires lie. In everyday life, our attention is usually on the shadows that are visible on the wall because our desire for being accepted by society is stronger than our desire for truth. Therefore, turning away from the wall towards truth without having the desire deep within would not bring us any closer to truth; not even if we followed other truth-seekers as part of a bigger fad, for instance, by practicing yoga, meditation, mindfulness, spirituality or personal development. We are usually only using these as tools to find temporary relief or to help us to go through a challenging situation rather than really be drawn to truth, even if we were convinced of the opposite. The same applies when showing great interest in exploring truth by reading books, attending meetings or going to retreats, but then not embodying the wisdom in our routine; that way, we would also not approach truth, but rather stay within the cave. However, once our desire lies in truth, we are ready to turn around completely and let go of everything that is of significance within the cave.

While the people in power seem to be one step ahead of the masses, they are still part of the ignorant ones because they are inside the cave. This group of opinion leaders includes people such as government officials, owners of companies, Nobel Prize winners, movie stars, musicians, religious leaders, gurus, teachers and to a certain degree parents. They manipulate the masses, including highly educated, smart and recognized people in ways that neither the ones manipulating nor the ones being manipulated are even aware of. They usually lack compassion and use the even more ignorant people to achieve their selfish goals. Furthermore, they dictate the values and morals in society and are even able to incite conflicts among different groups of people, if they wanted to. Ironically, the highest aspiration for many people is to become part of this seeming elite one day, not being aware that achieving this would keep them as far away from the truth as they are now. No matter our status, how much money or power we may have, we will never be ultimately happy or satisfied as long as we are in the cave; by nature, we always feel as if something were missing in life. In one way or another, everyone's nature is to live outside of the cave. Related to this, I once heard a *successful* person say something along the following lines: I wish everyone would be able to experience fame, have millions of dollars, have an amazing family, own the most beautiful villa and travel the world. By experiencing this so-called societal or material success, they would realize that nothing that society values has the power to make them ultimately happy or free.

The way out of the cave is to be dragged out by a force that rattles our current, seeming reality, which opens our minds and hearts to the bigger truth allowing us to challenge the status quo. In certain circumstances, this may be brought about by an accident, getting sick, a death of a close one – or in a less dramatic manner by realizing that *having the horses behind the carriage* has failed us again and again. This pathless path towards the unknown takes courage and may seemingly be hurtful because it is a process of letting go of the *old*, which we *falsely* identified with, not realizing that it just represents another layer of a *false* security. In other words, we *falsely* assume that the chains that force us to look at the wall were part of our identity, which could only happen because we forgot what it means to be free in the first place.

In the transition from the *dark* to the *light*, there is a high probability of being confused because it takes us some time to adjust to a new realm of reality. For instance, we may resonate with the statement that *the world is an illusion* and act according to our confusion, that is leaving everything behind to live the lifestyle of a hippie or a Sadhu. In such a case, we would confuse ignorance with truth because truth is not necessarily to be found by escaping from our current life. Or, some others may easily lose themselves on spiritual paths during that time of confusion without realizing it or even claiming to be on the one and only path to enlightenment. A good indication for being stuck in such confusion is when we hear spiritual leaders or gurus claim they have monopolized the one and only path to truth.

The people in power, and hence, also the *manipulated* masses, perceive the ones who have seen the truth as a *danger* to their power. Not only do they question the conventions and values of society, but also inspire people to challenge the status quo, that is, inspire them to think on their own. To defend their power, the opinion leaders do everything to discredit or ridicule the wise ones. When the source of this disrepute is an acknowledged authority, we take it to be true without hesitation, although when listening to our own intuition, we may agree with the wise ones because they directly speak to our heart. Yet, at the same time, we hesitate to talk about them or become like them because we are afraid to also get rejected by society. Having lost the ability to approach people and situations without having any prejudice, we listen more to authorities than to our own intuition. This shows that it is more important to us to belong to a *sick society* than to live in resonance with our own being. For instance, Socrates, one of the great Greek philosophers, was trialed, found guilty and executed one day for upsetting the opinion leaders by encouraging the people in society to question the conventional way of thinking and living.

When, after having experienced truth, going back to the cave to meet our friends and colleagues, they immediately notice that we look different, speak differently and act based on different values. What we used to be obsessed with is no longer relevant to us. For instance, if we played a game of jeopardy or tried to name as many things as possible reflected on the dark wall, we would no longer be good at it because for the most part of our life, our attention is now on the truth and not on something we would only use to impress others. In our new realm of reality, we do not submit to authorities anymore. We stop *reporting* to other people and no longer live by the preconceived limitations society, our managers, husbands and wives, boyfriends and girlfriends, or parents try to project onto us. Truth is our only guide, which makes our life authentic without trying to be something we are not. While thoughts may tell us that by doing so we would move further away from the people around us, in actuality, it is rather the other way around. We are united with all of life, more than ever before.

While discovering the depths of the cave allegory, it is essential to understand that we are never a victim of anything or anybody and that nothing in the world can ever affect or touch us deep down. Although we may act as if we were in the cave, we actually never left the light because our nature is, whether it may appear to us that way or not, truth itself. We can never enter the cave in actuality, but only seemingly so by identifying with what is happening within the dream. What we are at all times is not to be found within the dream, but in the one who is dreaming.

Now, the most eye-opening part for us is to question everything we have ever been told, not just when having a quiet moment, but especially in the moments, in which life is fully happening. It is important to understand that the intention is not to keep this on a theoretical level, but to let it impact our life from moment to moment. The point here is to see *how* we construct reality and *how* we come to certain conclusions about the world and not about its content. So, for instance, the question is not whether political party A or B is better or which perspective on the world is the best, but to understand what it *really* is that makes us think that political part A is better. Once we understand how reality is built from moment to moment, we are able to understand the essence of everything and are able to be fully alive, and no longer live to please others. That way, the constant suffering is replaced by light-heartedness, joy and true compassion.

I invite you to take a moment and see for yourself why you hate certain people, what makes you suffer and what you think of the world. What are your beliefs about yourself, the world and about how one should live life? See how you came to those beliefs in the first place. Are those your beliefs? Is it a product of society? How were you raised? Does it serve you and your life? Do you feel happy? What are the effects of your worldview and image about yourself on your daily activities? Question everything! Question what you have always been told to be true. Is it really true – even if media, your parents, teachers, and recognized people you admire say the same thing, which is contrary to what your intuition tells you? Understand what makes you believe what you believe. Does a particular belief bring you love or fear? Whose agenda is served by what you believe? How much do you listen to your inner voice or your intuition? Do not be attached to your reputation and be brutally honest with yourself while doing this life exercise.

Does your everyday desire lie more in trying to impress others or in truth?

Who or what is the ultimate instance you *report to* in your daily actions?

SPACE FOR INSPIRATION & CREATIVITY

MYTH 19 – SCHOOLS ARE MORE USEFUL THAN HARMFUL

It is no measure of health to be well-adjusted to a profoundly sick society.
– Krishnamurti, born in 1895

What we believe or seemingly experience to be true

Although we have doubts about certain aspects not really working in the education system – especially when seeing our children unhappy – we still send our children to school because it is common practice and in certain countries it even represents a law.

By and large, we think schools are useful because they help children to be accepted by society, find friends and eventually get a job. Students are told to be grateful for having the opportunity to go to school because there are many children in the world who are not privileged enough to receive this kind of conventional education. So, when students catch themselves complaining about having to go to school, they can calm those rebellious thoughts by being grateful for what they have.

Nonetheless, the very few people who have given this topic a deeper thought no longer resonate with the conventional education system, and as a result, have developed various, alternative education models, such as homeschooling or schools, in which students have the freedom to do whatever they fancy. Many of us are very hesitant to send our children to such alternative schools for many different reasons. When we are not sure about whom to listen to when it comes to educating our children, we think we cannot go wrong by just sticking to the proven, conventional way. That way, at least there is a high probability that our children do not stand out from the crowd, which we are sometimes afraid of.

When it comes to the more psychological and social aspects in school, we are astonished how much mobbing takes place and how nervous students are before taking exams. Students and parents are not really equipped with dealing with such difficult situations, and hence, in many instances, are forced to receive help from psychologists.

Some of the key assumptions behind the current education system are that children do not know much about life, do not have a strong intrinsic motivation to learn and tend to be lazy.

What may actually be happening

We can support setting children free if we teach them *how* to think and not *what* to think. Yet, what happens in school every day is exactly the opposite. Therefore, it is not enough to only improve or evolve the education system, but to completely reinvent it, starting from scratch. In a nutshell, what takes place in today's world with regard to education is the following: every day, we send our children to big concrete buildings, where they learn to be disciplined, obedient to authorities, afraid of failure, competitive and mean towards each other. They need to please and listen to teachers because they are at their mercy. We are usually not even aware of the strong conditioning taking place because we had been strongly conditioned in school ourselves, and hence, consider it as *common practice*. Conditioning children in school is highly effective because it shapes them at an age when they are most open to receive a doctrine. It has the power to impact how they see themselves and the world for the rest of their life. Also, we know when learning a certain skill before reaching puberty, such as learning a new language, we are able to speak it fluently and without any accent. Being conditioned before puberty has a similar strong effect on us. Think about it!

One would assume that learning as such would receive most attention by everyone being involved in school. But this is far from being the case. By far, the most important matter is to control whether students memorized something from a textbook or not. According to what we can observe in schools every day, the most effective way to conduct such a control is to ask students a few random questions about some pre-selected theories, pretending as if they were professional short-term memory players. It is more important for students to strengthen their short-term memory and learn *what* to think than to learn *how* to think and acquire other useful life skills. In so-called exams, students are not allowed to be creative or think for themselves, but instead have to cite what other people once said to meet the expectations of the teachers and the curriculum. So, it is not so much about becoming great at something, challenging the status quo and further developing in certain areas, but about maximizing discipline, memory and learning what they are told to. Therefore, school is the perfect instrument for bringing out *productive* entities, which is the best requisite for recruiting them to blindly grow the economy.

If parents or other opinion leaders, mostly through their own conditioning, have not already managed to take away all the children's creativity, openness and connection with their intuition, then schools come in and take care of the rest. After graduation, the young and *successful* adults easily conform to the standards and virtues of society, which the people currently in power are mostly interested in. What troubles them are rebels who are able to think on their own. And a society can only take a certain amount of troublemakers and freethinkers; if there were too many, the people currently in power would run into the risk of losing their power.

As we already touched upon, schools are not only *brainwashing* young people with regard to content, but also with regard to behavior. They reinforce competition rather than collaboration, obedience to authorities rather than freedom and pressure rather than creativity. In such an environment, students forget how to use their own talent and instead are forced to do things they do not resonate with. To understand this better, let's take a look at some of the virtues taught in school every day.

Discipline. To be disciplined means doing certain activities solely based on extrinsic motivation without an inner drive. Or put differently, it is about forcing oneself or others to do something in order to reach a certain desired outcome. It is not bad per se to engage in an activity to get something done here and there without an inner drive. But if this becomes a mindset, a life attitude or a habit for years, as it does in school or at work, then it has the ability to *enslave* us to activities, which is never healthy. In this regard, going to school for at least ten years with the goal of getting a degree, which is what nowadays every student mostly cares about, appears to be a modern form of *slavery* – but only if we are able to see this from an unconditioned point of view. Such a system can only work as long as most people in society are still unaware of what is going on, otherwise nobody would voluntarily go through such hardship or even have one's children go through this. It is as if it were an open secret veiled by our own conditioning.

Obedience. Obeying authorities means to do what others want us to do while ignoring our inner resonance. It is also about suppressing what we desire, which we do because we are afraid of facing negative consequences. After obeying teachers for more than ten years, obeying all kind of people becomes second nature to us. We obey government officials, managers and partners forgetting what it means to follow our intuition, think on our own and healthily question authorities. This is equivalent to an inner giving up with regard to what we truly stand for, which no longer allows us to follow our dreams. As a result, most students do not really know what they want to do after graduation, but instead pursue a career that is valued by society.

Fear and pressure. Learning to be fearful in this context means to be put under constant pressure to perform. When our performance does not meet certain expectations, we face highly negative consequences. For instance, since I was mentally strong in my teens, this constant pressure helped me to exceed versus others, whether it was in tennis or school. I was not nervous before exams while most of my classmates were devastated. Playing competitive tennis helped me immensely to mentally deal with pressure, emotions, winning and losing. As practical as this may be in dealing with competitive situations in society, I felt I lost touch with spontaneity, feelings, intuition and compassion towards others and even myself. I had built thick walls blocking me from negative, but also positive influences – and even from the *life juice* itself. I had become empty and numb inside. Being mentally tough had not only become a tool I would use in certain situations, but an attitude towards life, which made me more independent, but at the same time more *lonely* because I disconnected myself from what was happening right in front of me – something called life. But I only realized this after I started my first job. The more I spent time in places such as India, Cambodia and Bali, the more I realized how tough and strong-minded people in the West tend to be and how soft and *heart-centered* people in Asia can be. Only when mistaking an environment characterized by pressure for a given reality, we feel we need to be strong in order not to get run over by others. But life does not require us to be strong. Life as such is soft and we can fully open up towards it without having to build walls. The more we close ourselves, the harder life seems to become.

Dead knowledge. In our society, we value *dead* knowledge significantly more than *living* knowledge. Dead knowledge is the knowledge of naming things. It is knowledge that originates from other thoughts, that is, memory, which is isolated from our intuition and from first-hand experience. We acquire *dead* knowledge from newspapers, television, books, magazines and so on. Such knowledge is *dead* because it stays purely in the realm of thoughts without us embodying it. We just *carry* it around in our memories without having experienced or truly felt it ourselves. *Dead* knowledge can be easily put into words and is transferable to others because it originated to us that way in the first place. On the contrary, *living* knowledge always comes from first-hand experience. It is *hard* to find the right words for it and many times even impossible for others to understand. But it is the knowledge that represents the basis for us to be in touch with where life is actually happening. An example will illustrate the difference between the two. Let's assume a teacher lectures about Hinduism, the main religion in India, and knows almost everything about its essential aspects such as its rituals, Gods, holy festivals and the meaning of the caste system. He is also able to name everything, to talk about it with great confidence and to philosophize about it. Yet, the source of his knowledge is purely from books and other media since he neither practices Hinduism nor has he ever visited India, where he would be in touch with people practicing it. He is only able to teach it from the perspective of a non-Hindu. He would not know how it feels to be Hindu, and what deeper meaning the rituals have on a feeling level. Hence, he teaches *dead* knowledge based on second-hand information. The teaching would only come to life if he had experienced everything he talks about himself. In another example, *dead* knowledge is as if we knew the menu of a restaurant by heart and already spoke to many people who have enjoyed various of the meals and drinks, but never tasted any of the items on the menu ourselves. On the contrary, *living* knowledge would mean we actually taste the food and the drinks and tell others about it from our first-hand experience.

Interestingly, since first-hand information varies from person to person – because we give everything all the meaning it has – it actually makes a standard teaching impossible. Thus, conventional schools are not an appropriate platform to teach first-hand wisdom to students. There is no such thing as right and wrong in *living* knowledge and no exam would ever be able to serve to control whether we successfully learned something or not. Only *dead* knowledge can be taught in a standardized way, which is *celebrated* in school every day. In the conventional system, all children are treated in the same way, as if they were dragged through the education system on an assembly line. This is not only true for the main subjects they engage in, but also the way the subjects are taught. Students are treated like empty containers or machines that need to be filled with knowledge, and are not allowed to bring in their whole human side including their feelings.

In schools today, children are taught about an imaginary and projected world, which they are forced to believe and understand, although the image of that world is radically distorted. Schools teach us about a violent, cruel, cold and scarce world full of problems. Lacking the ability to challenge the status quo, we agree to the wrong assumption that there is an objective world out there – which, by the way, is explored in more detail under *Myth 10*. We never take the time to sincerely question whether the world as such is actually cruel and cold or whether it is us bringing in that cruelty by giving it that meaning, and as a consequence, preparing for it while everybody else around us is doing the same. We believe everything we are told because everyone around us including media, experts, governments, friends and parents confirm that same image of the world. Sooner or later, we give in, play along and even advocate this seeming reality. Imagine Galileo were a student telling his teacher the world is not flat. Not only would he get a bad grade, but may even be labeled *crazy*. Is that really how we want our children to grow up? Does this help them to prepare to become free or rather a highly productive *slave* within a greedy society?

The assumption that human beings are only willing to learn when they are forced to, on which our education system is based on, is obviously not valid. We are only not willing to learn when we are put under pressure, are forced to learn something we are not interested in or are asked to obey authorities, which makes many students react in a seemingly rebellious or sullen way. Otherwise, learning is second nature to us and we are eager to constantly develop. Funnily enough, the difference between *good* and *bad* students is almost never their mind capacity, but how strong their desire is to learn. Have you ever asked yourself why children are forced to learn? Did someone force us to walk or talk when we were children or did it happen naturally?

So, what is there for us to do? First of all, it is essential to understand that nobody in this discussion is to be blamed. The lack is not to be found in certain groups of people, such as teachers, parents, government leaders or students. But it is rather that as a collective we have forgotten how to think freely and how to challenge the status quo. Furthermore, we are intentionally not proposing a new education system here. Because if we did, we would just put it on top of the current one mixing it with the current state of mind of the people. There are many solutions one could implement, but the first and most important step is to understand in full depth what is currently happening to our children and to what extent we still *brainwash* and condition them. It is essential to understand the current situation both on the inside and the outside.

Until we are not fully aware of the real problem, no radical change will follow, no matter how many seemingly great actions or solutions we would propose or implement. The desired revolution will only be brought to life by people who themselves are free and fully alive, in the sense of embodying human virtues such as sincerity, authenticity and compassion. When we send children to conventional schools, we seemingly adjust them to the status quo of society, and when we homeschool them, we adjust them to the status quo of their parents. But when we have *teachers* who embody freedom, they learn how to be free. That way, we allow children to learn life skills such as *Challenging the status quo*, Practicing *compassion*, Seeing how *awareness allows change*, *Dealing with emotions* or *Understanding we are not separate from each other*.

When starting a school completely from scratch, how would you organize it for children to be truly free?

What are you very good at and where and how did you learn those skills?

SPACE FOR INSPIRATION & CREATIVITY

MYTH 20 – DEVELOPED COUNTRIES ARE MORE DEVELOPED THAN DEVELOPING COUNTRIES

I cannot teach anybody anything,
I can only make them think.
– Socrates, born in 469 BC

What we believe or seemingly experience to be true

We believe it is useful to economically separate the world into so-called developed, emerging and developing countries. This segmentation helps governments and global organizations to negotiate trade agreements between strategically important countries, design aid programs for developing countries, and, in a broader sense, create a more economically balanced world.

Within global organizations such as the United Nations or the World Trade Organization, developed countries have significantly more power and influence over world affairs than countries with small overall and military budgets. The richest countries maintain their own *clubs* and regular meetings, in which the key objectives are not necessarily to help economically poor countries as it is usually portrayed in media, but to discuss how they can become even more powerful and richer in the name of providing aid to developing countries. Most often, the true beneficiaries behind this are not directly governments or global organizations, but obviously a few powerful corporations, families or lobbyists pulling the strings in the background.

In the minds of the people, the given country or market segmentation is not perceived as something only limited to macroeconomic issues, but also merges into social and even psychological matters. People from developed countries may somehow get the impression they are *better* than the ones from emerging or developing countries because of the higher standard of living and stronger monetary and military power existing in their country. This is similar to people or families believing they are superior to others because they have a bigger house, a better car or a higher-paying job. Likewise, in an underlying way, people from developing countries often feel inferior when meeting people from developed countries.

What may actually be happening

While so-called developed countries may be advanced in terms of economical strength, standard of living and ability to assert and influence others, they are mostly *underdeveloped* in true human virtues and psychological skills, such as being free, living in harmony with nature, living a happy and peaceful life in the community and leaving other nations in peace. The *deprioritization* of human virtues is the flipside of their economic progress. *Tokenistically*, while developed countries do engage in attempting to solve environmental and human rights issues, major conflicts and epidemic, they are usually also the ones causing the misery in the first place. For instance, developed countries do much harm to the rest of the world by being arrogant enough to try to convert other nations to live by their ideals, many times in the name of something they do not even live by themselves, that is *democracy*. While this activism helps them to further grow economically and cope with the immense pressure to continuously grow their Gross Domestic Product, which every country is confronted with, their efforts to then help *at the end of the chain* are merely a drop in the ocean and mainly serve to establish a better reputation in public and calm the masses to avoid a revolution.

In developed countries, the masses are highly prone to being *brainwashed* in many different ways. Believing they can *buy* happiness is one of the results of this. To understand the extent of the latter, it is enough to observe people in stores during pre-Christmas season or on *Black Friday* when they literally fight each other over buying products. They have forgotten how to think on their own and how to not blindly obey or conform to authorities, which are factors making them psychologically underdeveloped. People give away their power very easily, which is one of the reasons brainwashing works so effectively. This again is used to full capacity by big corporations influencing them in a substantial way through their products and advertising campaigns, which, by the way, are psychological masterpieces in terms of manipulating people. At the same time, the masses are distracted and kept numb through entertainment, fighting with their neighbors and friends, being obsessed with sex, chasing happiness in relationships and objects, climbing career ladders and feeling guilty. Interestingly, the stronger the masses in a certain country are brainwashed, the more economically developed the country usually is. In such countries, people learn to obey in the highest manner, and hence, serve as immensely productive resources without even being aware that they give away their freedom and are exploited. Paradoxically, they even believe they are more important than the people who are not as productive because the reward system values and remunerates them for their productive behavior. This system is set up in such a brilliant way keeping people *enslaved* and it will continue to work smoothly as long as the masses stay unaware of its underlying mechanisms.

Another example showing how prone the masses in the developed countries are to brainwashing is how they have stood on the sidelines during the so-called chemical revolution. At some point in the twentieth century, it was *hip and cool* to no longer cure sickness naturally as it was the case for millions of years, but to consume chemicals in form of pills, injections, lotions and so on. Many decades ago, big corporations foresaw a big financial opportunity in bringing more chemical products to households, and as a result, chemical ingredients are part of most products they consume on a daily basis today, without even fully understanding their long-term side effects. Chemicals can be found in products related to food, health, beauty, textiles and many more. For most of them, this chemical revolution and the amounts of chemicals they put in their body only seem to become problematic when encountering major sickness or accidents in their family, among friends or in themselves. In a way, it seems chemicals have even become part of their natural environment because they no longer remember a world without them. Through the span of only three to four generations, they have come thus far that they have become psychologically and physiologically dependent on chemicals. While their children do not know which plants can help their body to initiate self-healing anymore, they are now able to name many pharmaceutical brands or products.

Furthermore, in developed countries, they are also underdeveloped when it comes to the way the masses live together in communities. They are taught to be as independent as possible, ideally not having to rely on others for anything. For instance, instead of talking about problems with family and friends, they buy consulting services from so-called professionals who have acquired certificates. Many times, they are too afraid to talk about their problems with friends or colleagues because they are afraid of showing vulnerability and of being judged. In contrast, coaches or psychologists are still mostly redundant in developing countries such as India or Indonesia today. Those professions are still foreign expressions to most. Instead of seeking help from professionals, people in those countries still find support among friends and family to get over problems. Or they seek help from someone in the community who specializes in a certain field of expertise applying living knowledge transmitted through his or her ancestors over the course of several generations, which includes people such as healers, astrologers and medicine men.

While so-called developing and emerging countries may not be perfect, there are many aspects people from developed countries can still learn from them with regard to human virtues. *Still*, because many of them have already started to be taken over by the same greed one finds in developed countries – especially those countries that promise fast and relatively easy economic growth, such as India, China, Brazil and Russia. For instance, people in developing and emerging countries are still much more connected to nature with regard to healing, nutrition and seeing it as something alive. They treat nature not as *dead matter* or something they own – as it is the case in developed countries – but with dignity and compassion. Furthermore, while people in developed countries always run from one appointment to the next, children even included nowadays, people in developing countries still value rest, patience and the beauty and simplicity of the moment, where the actual *magic* that each one is looking for happens. This is partly due to the fact that conceptual thinking in those nations is traditionally not given the same importance as in industrialized countries. As a consequence, while people in developed countries seem to be glued to the thought process, heavily regretting the past and being worried about the future, people in developing countries still show more signs of presence and being connected with their intuition and more subtle energies. For instance, this becomes obvious when looking at people's faces in developing countries, which, for the most part, are full of life.

The point here is not to generalize or point fingers at certain people, countries or organizations, but to see that people from developed countries can immensely learn from so-called developing countries with regard to human virtues. At the same time, there are many aspects they can learn from developed countries, such as increasing the standard of living in a healthy and organic way using sustainable technologies; but without the unpleasant aftertaste of people from developed countries projecting onto them how they should live their life. Sometimes, it is good to be reminded that being wealthy and greedy does not make people from the West any better than people who treat nature as their friend and see not economic growth, but human touch and holistic happiness as a decent goal of humanity.

How many chemicals are you consuming every day and what effects do they have on your body and wellbeing?

....

....

....

....

....

Are there any people out there who are better than others in their essence? Why or why not?

....

....

....

....

....

SPACE FOR INSPIRATION & CREATIVITY

6

You are happy –
whether with or without
your partner

MYTH 21 – I OWN MY PARTNER

Let the lover be disgraceful, crazy, absent-minded.
Someone sober will worry about events going badly.
Let the lover be.
– Rumi, born in 1207

What we believe or seemingly experience to be true

We talk to or treat our boyfriends, girlfriends, husbands, wives, children or family members as if we owned them. Somehow, we think we have the right to check whom they meet, to whom they speak and whom they message. Since we want the best for them, we tell them what point of view they should have, how they should live their life, what they should think and how they should treat us.

When meeting a significant other at first, there are no signs of ownership, yet. But the longer we know someone and the longer we live together, the more this sense of ownership develops – also because we are suspicious and afraid that they may leave us one day. As a consequence, we are jealous when our partner meets or spends time with certain other beautiful or successful people; also because in secret we are worried they may like them more than us. Trying to avoid imaginary worst-case scenarios, we live by the motto *trust is good, control is better*.

Since we have this sense of ownership, we set high expectations for our partners with regard to how they are supposed to behave, squeeze toothpaste, cook or speak to others; the list is endless. It also results in taking our partners for granted, which is demonstrated by actions such as no longer holding the door open for them, no longer being grateful for having them in our life or neither seeing nor appreciating what they do for us every day.

What may actually be happening

The open secret to a healthy relationship is to give one's partner full freedom as to who they are and what they do without imposing any restrictions upon them – in the same way we give someone full freedom when meeting him or her for the very first time. The more we try to control our partner and the more we emotionally and psychologically claim him or her to be ours, the more light-heartedness and beauty we take out of the relationship. Since our seeming need to control others usually springs from the fear of getting disappointed or hurt, we put both, our partners and us, into a low-spirited energy – us by being afraid and others by imposing our fear upon them.

The sense of ownership is either brought in by at least one of the partners or is developed and maintained in low-spirited relationships. Every relationship is tilted either more towards an uplifting or low-spirited dynamic. While the uplifting dynamic is characterized by giving each other energy, the low-spirited one is characterized by using the relationship to try to fill a lack inside. At the same time, in every relationship, there are phases that are more uplifting and again phases that are more low-spirited. But what counts is its core underlying dynamic. Take a moment to reflect on the dynamics of your relationships with the people close to you. Which ones are generally tilted more towards uplifting and which ones towards low-spirited energies? Which relationships give you and which ones take away energy? Look beyond what meets the eye.

We are not always aware of a sense of ownership being present in a relationship because it can occur that a low-spirited relationship is packaged as inspirational to at least one of the partners. For instance, let's assume Olivia is in love with Liam. She highly admires him for being a very handsome and wise man. When spending time with him, Olivia finds herself in extremely uplifting moods, and when being away from him, she misses him very much because it feels as if he had become part of her. He somewhat notices that she is strongly attached to him, but is not fully aware of it and somehow prefers not to let it come to his awareness. He enjoys spending time with her because he appreciates her appearance, sweetness and softness, but is overwhelmed by her emotional attachment. To him, it feels as if the relationship were rather imbalanced because he is not as attached to her as she is to him. But he still holds on to the relationship, also because he is accustomed to being in it and he would not know how his life would be without her. Also, he would not want to hurt his partner by, for instance, breaking up with her. To her, however, the relationship appears to be highly balanced because she regularly convinces herself that he is also happy with her. Olivia is submissive to Liam, while Liam enjoys having emotional control over Olivia in secret, both being unaware of this.

Overall such a relationship is usually low-spirited for both parties for several reasons. First of all, after the initial feeling *head over heals in love* phase, both of them abstract a certain degree of beauty from the relationship by establishing a sense of ownership and respective expectations that come along with that. On an emotional level, Olivia expects Liam to uplift her and Liam expects Olivia to be submissive. Secondly, both of them either entered or stay in the relationship to benefit from it. Olivia entered it to experience uplifting states, enjoying moods similar to when a fan meets her idol, and Liam stays in the relationship to enjoy all the attention he receives from her making him almost feel like a *star,* to which he has become emotionally attached. Thirdly, despite both of them having the intuition of the relationship not being healthy for them, they hold on to it very strongly due to their respective fears of potentially losing or hurting each other. Sooner or later, this manifests either in form of a hurtful breakup or a numb relationship based on compromise. Although at first a certain relationship may appear to be uplifting, we are often not aware of all the underlying aspects described above, and hence, enter or stay in a negative spiral, which may last for years or for some even *till death us do part.* We could avoid all this hardship by listening more to and radically following our intuition.

In contrast, in a truly uplifting relationship, neither of the partners expects to benefit from it, neither on the levels we are aware of nor on the ones we are not aware of. Uplifting relationships are based on primal trust, not on any kind of vibrations of control or ownership. To fully trust our partner, we first need to be able to trust life and ourselves because we are the ones bringing it into relationships. Furthermore, we are ready for a sincere, truly uplifting and lasting relationship when we do not bring any deeper problems with us and mistakenly believe the relationship will be able to make us happy.

We do not actually change others or relationships by *trying* to change them, which is usually the first thing that comes to our mind, but by purely changing our perspective, attitude and behavior towards them. For instance, if we were to find ourselves in a relationship, in which we felt that our partner treats us as if he or she owned us, it would be enough to be aware of the underlying mechanism and start being the change we would like to see in our partner. This means we would give him or her full freedom and would not feed or react to any kind of behavior from his or her side whenever he or she approaches us with a sense of ownership. On an energetic and emotional level, our partner would eventually adjust to our behavior because the previous one is no longer fed through our reactions and resistance. I invite you not to agree or disagree with what is written here. Just see and validate it for yourself relying on your experience and not on your current or past beliefs.

A good indication for the harm we do when exercising a sense of ownership is to look at what we as modern humanity do to nature and animals. On the one hand, there are cultures or peoples who treat nature, our planet and animals as if they owned them. As a result, it is accepted to exploit resources, use oceans as waste bins and massively torture animals. On the other hand, there are people who treat nature and animals as part of them, and hence, treat them with dignity and compassion. The same principle applies to our partnerships.

Going a step further, at the end of the day, we treat our partners in the same manner as we treat ourselves including all the *good* and all the *bad* aspects. And since most of us sense a deep lack within, we usually treat others from that lack, that is, in a rather *nasty* way, too, without really being aware of it. The closer we are to others, the more we are ourselves and the harsher we usually are – unless we have learned to be kind to ourselves.

Going again a step further, it is essential to see that we do not even *own* ourselves. What do we mean by that? It means we do not own a body, emotions and thoughts, but they are part of the whole. That way, instead of putting us down and being harsh to ourselves, we are able to learn to be grateful and show compassion and dignity even towards *our* body, feelings and behavior. By becoming aware of this, we automatically change others around us and make the world, as we perceive it, a better place. The beauty of a bird does not lie in imprisoning it in a cage, but in letting it fly in unconditional freedom.

What gives you the right to tell your partner what to do and what not to do every day?

What fears are you projecting onto your partner?

SPACE FOR INSPIRATION & CREATIVITY

MYTH 22 – MY PARTNER GETS BORING OVER TIME

The supreme state of human love is... the unity of one soul in two bodies.
– Aurobindo, born in 1872

What we believe or seemingly experience to be true

When entering a new relationship, starting a new job, or moving to our dream city, we are usually all excited feeling as if everything were perfect in one way or another.

After some time, though – which may be anywhere between two days and five years – we come to a point, at which our excitement reduces. Some may refer to this phenomenon as *reality is striking back.* As a consequence, small things start to bother us, such as our partner leaving his or her clothes on the floor, not leaving behind the sink in a clean manner, randomly placing plates and mugs, provoking us unnecessarily or no longer holding the door open for us. Or, he or she intentionally says things or behaves in ways that we do not approve. All of this gives us the impression that he or she does not care about us anymore.

Our first reaction to this is usually to think that our partner has significantly changed since the moment we first met, for which we find enough proof using our memory. Even after confronting our partner about certain issues again and again, he or she still does not significantly improve his or her behavior towards us, which in many instances results in the relationship eventually coming to an end. On a rational level, we are usually convinced that the cause for the breakup is found in our partner's behavior, although in our next relationships the same pattern repeats over and over again. Being occupied dealing with strong emotions, we do not even have the time and energy to question what may actually be the underlying cause for our relationships not working out. Therefore, the question arises whether it is possible to experience the initial excitement that we undergo when encountering something new not only as a temporary feeling, but also as a constant joy in relationships and in life in general.

What may actually be happening

The simple answer to this question is: yes, it is possible. Since the answer may not be in line with our everyday experience, but still resonates within us on a deeper level, let's take a look at what happens between this all-amazing beginning and the phase characterized by mutual annoyance. Is it always our partner who changes? Or maybe, did we change our behavior towards our partner? Or could it be that our perception plays a major role in this? What is the overarching pattern? On the one hand, when meeting new people or experiencing new situations, why is it that we feel excited and open-minded, and on the other hand, when things become more familiar, or we label them as *I know* or *Seen this, done that*, we lose the ability to wonder or to be innocently excited?

When experiencing something new, such as new countries, songs, people, partners, books or movies, we are usually in an open-minded and uplifting state – unless we are so strongly conditioned that we are not even able to be open to anything anymore, which may apply to very few of us. This open-minded state is characterized by an absence of comparison, an absence of a strong reference point to something *known*, and experiencing objects more with our *hearts* than with our minds. Being open-minded, we see objects more as they really are without making associations to the past and the future. This way, we have the mindset of *not knowing* or *not naming things*, that is, we experience the purity of what is happening, which enables our attention to be in the moment itself. It even seems as if the concept of time no longer existed. As soon as we claim we know someone or something, the object or person becomes a *dead* thing, or to be more precise, is reduced to a mere image. Out of habit, we easily mistake an image, that is a mental representation, for the object or person himself. When interacting with an image of someone instead of interacting with what is actually in front of us, we do not allow life to flow through – neither on our nor on their side. The main difference between experiencing something *new* versus *old* is not so much in the people or occasions we experience – what we would usually assume – but rather in how we perceive them.

To illustrate this, let's take a look at what happens when meeting a beautiful woman. When seeing her at first, we may be very impressed by her charisma, looks, confidence and style. At such a moment, we are extremely excited and would like to spend more time with her. However, the more we get to know her, the more we forget what it is that impressed us at first, and the more we try to throw our net of thoughts at her trying to grasp the essence of what it is that makes her so special. And the more we do so through comparing, judging and knowing, the more beauty we suck out of her, up to a point, at which there are no longer two people meeting in spontaneity and openness, but instead two images boring each other. In contrast, in the beginning, we do not have any image of her, but rather directly experience her *perfume* made of a feeling of *wow*. This very feeling of *wow* allows us to see her for who she is. But after a few encounters, we no longer see what is in front of our eyes because we are too busy interacting with the image we have created of her. Having an image of someone or something puts us into a narrow-minded state, characterized by a routine, in which we do not perceive anything as truly beautiful anymore. Seeing the world through such a perspective makes us feel numb and empty because we encounter our old memories and images of others rather than fully experiencing life in the timeless moment. At the same time, though, we are never a victim of other people or circumstances, but, simply put, have the immense power in us to perceive everything in life as beautiful, boring or whatever else we want to see. However, this applies only as long as we are aware of this underlying mechanism.

I invite you to take a minute to reflect on the relationships you have with your mother, your father, your sister, your brother, your partner, your manager or your friend. For instance, when being around your partner, do you treat him based on what he did to you in the past, or purely based on what you experience right in front of you using your perceptions? What difference do you observe? When do you feel more light-hearted and when more disappointed? I further invite you to do the exercise of pretending to only *know* what you experience with your senses – as opposed to using your memory, which we do most of the times. See what happens to you and the other person the next time you meet. What we can say for sure is that life will become lighter. And you will also notice that others change, simply because they are not isolated from your perceptions. See it for yourself. Nobody else can do this for you.

Since it plays a major role in how we relate to others, let's take a closer look at that, which observes and interprets what is happening, that is us. In quantum physics, it is stated that the observer has the biggest impact on any experiment, while before in classic physics, the observer had been completely ignored due to the assumption that there is an objective world *out there* separate from us. When applying this principle from quantum physics to how we relate to others, what exactly does it implicate? Why do we say it has the biggest impact on the relationship? We are the one who observes our partner and ourselves and nothing can ever take place outside of our observation, which, at the same time means that we give everything all the meaning it has. For instance, let's assume my partner is late for an anniversary dinner and I get really upset at her because I interpret her being late in one of the following ways: she does not care about me, she takes me for granted, she recently has not shown or expressed that she loves me, she may cheat on me and so on. It is not really her behavior that gets me upset, but my own interpretation and feelings triggered by her behavior. On a deeper level, this interpretation is linked to my insecurities and fear, such as the fear of being abandoned, the fear of being alone or the fear of not being good enough. 99.9 percent of the time, we are worried or get upset about circumstances that will never even happen – this occurs because we listen to thoughts as if our life depended on them. See it for yourself. Think of everything you have ever been worried about and of what actually happened in your life; you will quickly see that the vast majority of worries were just a *waste* of energy. When being aware of this, the power is with us with regard to whether or not we are able to rest during a dinner with our partner, fully enjoy a music concert or feel at peace in our relationship in general. No event will ever again have the power to disturb our peace of mind because it is not about the events taking place, but about the thoughts and feelings about those events that we cling on to or not. This awareness opens doors for us unveiling a world, in which we are able to fully enjoy life for what it really is without getting distracted by some temporary *noise*.

When seemingly being hurt by our partners, we usually act as if they intentionally wanted to hurt us. With regard to any of our relationships, it is essential to understand that people do not intent to hurt others. They are too focused and obsessed with themselves to spend time on making and executing a plan to hurt others. What happens instead is that they follow their self-interest, which in certain instances happens not to be in line with our interest, and hence, seemingly hurts us. Seeing this clearly will make the process of forgiving our friends and partner significantly faster and easier.

What contributes to and even accelerates conflicts with our partner or friends is the following common attitude: *if you do not treat me nicely, I also won't treat you nicely*, and hence, we create an extremely negative spiral effect in a relationship. Such an attitude can even become the underlying dynamic of a relationship. It usually starts with one of the partners or friends experiencing a first, unsettled disappointment, which in turn makes the one being hurt unconsciously wanting to hurt the other, which takes the relationship into a negative spiral. From then on, we start treating our partner based on what he or she did or did not do to us instead of acting from a place of compassion and innocence. When being unaware of this dynamic, it can ruin a relationship. Alternatively, being aware of this mechanism can help to bring back an uplifting spin to the relationship, especially when we are ready to take the first step to settle the underlying conflict and not wait for our partner to do so. What is true for a negative spiral effect is also true for a positive one. When someone treats us in an unexpectedly warm-hearted way, we treat her in the same way in return because it makes us feel special and uplifting.

The topic of relationships is also highly interesting when looking at what happens on an energy level. Every *body* sends out certain vibrational frequencies that differ from body to body and either do or do not resonate with ours. Put differently, while some people uplift us, some others put us down energetically; but of course only as long as we allow this to happen. When two people romantically meet at first, they usually feel a high attraction towards each other. The more time they spend with each other, especially when sleeping together in the same bed over a longer period of time, the more their body frequencies adjust to each other. While the result of having similar frequencies may provide them with a feeling of familiarity and security, the couple's physical attraction to each other gradually reduces because it is more of the same or more of the known. This is also why it is very attractive for people to have an affair – they are energetically highly attracted by people with certain body frequencies different from their own. And this is the main factor we are attracted to certain people in the first place; the main underlying element is not necessarily the looks or character, as we would usually assume, but the underlying resonating vibrational frequencies of the bodies. When living together for a longer period of time, another effect of the alignment of the body frequencies is that the need to speak to each other reduces. Words are no longer needed in many situations because the partners energetically become very familiar with what the other person feels or thinks. The same applies to dog owners who supposedly start to look like their dogs. They obviously do not actually *look* like them, but they acquire a very similar body frequency, which makes some people say they *look* alike.

Now it is up to you. On the one hand, you can continue to *lock up* your partner and friends using the mindset of *I know*, with the consequence of coming across nothing but empty, boring and *dead* objects and situations. Or, on the other hand, you can be fully alive experiencing people and situations from an embodied open-mindedness that does not know separation. It is about meeting people without being attached to labeling them or to what happened in the past, and purely seeing what appears right in front of you. The more your interest of attention moves from your head to your heart, the more you notice that you have more in common with others than what differentiates you. You will recognize your own essence in others and your relationships will stop being so mechanical. What are you waiting for? The good news is you do not have to wait for your partner to change first, but you have all the power to change the people around you by experiencing them anew from moment to moment. You, as the observer of everything, have all the power. I invite you not to think about why this may be or may not be so, but instead experience it for yourself right now. Your partner and the world are only as good and beautiful as you allow them to be!

How does it make you feel when seeing something wonderful for the very first time??

Let go of the image you have of yourself or of close friends and see them anew every time you meet. What changes do you observe?

SPACE FOR INSPIRATION & CREATIVITY

EPILOGUE

Inquirer: I understand most of what is covered in this book intellectually, but it is not my actual experience. What can I do to implement it in my everyday life?

Ramakrishna: I invite you to entertain the possibility that it may be the other way around. Your actual experience is that of a formless, indefinable and untouchable essence whose nature is inherent joy that is not of this world. What keeps you seemingly away from fully experiencing this is the belief that you are not that. You will never be able to become what you already are – neither by thinking nor by any other means, no matter how hardworking, disciplined or diligent you may be.

Inquirer: Is it not better to follow a few concrete steps than just becoming aware of certain mechanisms?

Ramakrishna: Giving someone certain steps to follow is as if a doctor gave you crutches without treating your leg injury. It would make your life more convenient, but it would not heal the wound. Additionally, let's assume you have a few hidden, dirty spots and corners in your house. The reason you have not cleaned those is that you are not aware of the dirt. But as soon as you saw the dirt, you would naturally clean it. Instead, if you applied the most sophisticated cleaning methods in the market without seeing the dirt, you may feel you do everything you can, but you would not see any significant effect.

SPACE FOR INSPIRATION & CREATIVITY

SPACE FOR INSPIRATION & CREATIVITY

SPACE FOR INSPIRATION & CREATIVITY

POSTSCRIPT

On the following pages, I briefly summarize some of the essential points that are described in more detail throughout this book. For many of us, staying open-minded to something we do not necessarily agree with at first on a thinking or feeling level is not easy because of our strong identification with acquired thoughts, judgments and comparisons. It is not about agreeing or disagreeing with what is written here, but about being open to discover for yourself what it means to be fully alive. Before presenting the respective concepts, it is noteworthy that our essence is not to be found through understanding what we are, but instead, it reveals itself once we understand what we are *not*.

We are not a long-lasting, independent, separate entity. Starting at the age of around two, we acquire the belief that we are individuals separated from everything else. From that point on, we successfully collect seeming evidence to validate this belief in every situation we face. However, what we mistake for an entity is merely a construct consisting of a body and a conceptual reference point or a seeming control center within the realm of thinking and feeling, which does not have a separate reality on its own. There is only one entity in this life, which is not the sum of all bodies and reference points, but the one and the same omnipresent intelligence giving birth to the world from moment to moment. In some spiritual, yogic or self-improvement circles, we frequently hear phrases such as *We are all one.* While many of us intuitively resonate with this statement, it is hard to grasp because we look for this oneness – the formless – in the world of objects – the form. We try to become the formless, that is, our essence, as the form, that is, our body and thinking, forgetting that we are already the formless. In other words, the object pretends to be the subject. From the perspective of an object, the statement *we are all one* does not make any sense because as soon as we pretend to be a separate individual, we cannot be one with all; at best maybe connected with all. But when realizing we are one with everything by nature – in the realm of the formless – there is no longer even the need to be connected because we are closer to everyone and everything than any connection will ever be able to take us. Clearly seeing that we are not a long-lasting, separate entity would already be enough to completely transform our life.

We are not the doer, thinker or decision maker. The obvious consequence of not being a separate entity is that we are also not in control of circumstances and events, at least not from the seeming perspective of being a body or a separate individual. Not being the doer includes all activities, including breathing, thinking, doing and singing, which we usually assume we would be in control of. What happens instead is the following: events and activities occur, and in form of an afterthought, our thought-constructed reference center claims that *it* was the one thinking and doing, that is, it claims to be the thinker and doer right after each particular activity takes place.

We are not our body. There are billions of human bodies in this world, but we are neither a body nor located in a body. Identifying with and acting as a body makes all of our relationships with others, nature and the world highly mechanical because, in such a case, relationships are merely interactions between two superficial objects. By mistaking the body for a subject, we overlook that even the body is part of the world of objects. The moment we recognize that the subject is not in the body, we are able to see what may actually be happening. Since the body is an object itself, it is not the one that is aware of and senses objects. What we truly are is the intelligent, formless *subject*. The body is merely an instrument we use to be in touch with the world of objects. Being identified with an instrument is not only very limiting, but is also the cause for our almost constant suffering. Furthermore, since it is possible to replace broken organs, such as an eye, with the ones of another body and still have the same seeming sense of *I*, it shows that what we are cannot be the body.

We are not our thinking. The older we get, the more our attention is directed to the thought stream, which at some point, even becomes an almost constant condition. Not only have we started to listen to thoughts as if they were our *masters*, but also even started to identify with them. As a result of being enslaved to our thoughts, our self-worth depends on what we think. When negative thoughts occur, we feel down and when positive ones occur, we feel happy. As soon as we realize we are not our thoughts and the thoughts are not from or about us, we lose interest in following them and are able to find true rest. That way, it is finally possible to use thoughts as an effective tool. The problem is never the thoughts themselves, but our attachment to and obsession with them. Mindfulness and mediation exercises may help to get temporary relief from thoughts, but are not enough to lose interest in them.

We are not our feelings. Similar to the way we heavily *consume* thoughts, we are also obsessed with feelings. We push away uncomfortable feelings and try to get more of the pleasant ones. We even structure and plan our life according to the latter, which restricts us in many ways. When we are identified with or afraid of certain feelings, we no longer have a healthy relationship with them. Only when we understand that feelings are neither *good* nor *bad*, but have the function of helping us to navigate through life, we allow our relationship with them to change. The nature of feelings is to come and go like clouds. Therefore, when a sad feeling shows up, we fully embrace it, and as a result, it naturally disappears again without leaving any trace.

We are not the form, but the formless. Form includes everything that is perceivable including bodies, objects, thoughts, feelings and subtle energies. Since we are able to perceive or be aware of form, it is impossible for us to be the same. Imagine your tongue was made of salt and I put salt on your tongue. Would you be able to taste it? No, because it is not possible to perceive anything that is made of the same substance. We always have to be outside of or different from something to be able to perceive it. Form can be defined, labeled, perceived, argued about, liked or disliked and accepted or rejected. But the formless, what we are, cannot be grasped by any means, neither by our senses, nor by our thoughts nor by anything else.

There are not two kinds of selves. Sometimes we may hear that there is a self and a higher self, or an ego and a higher self. Again, there are not two entities in this life. The ego or the self that some refer to are not entities in themselves, but merely a bundle of thoughts, feelings and memories. If we assumed there were two kinds of selves, it would put us on a never-ending path towards becoming a higher self without realizing that we already are what we are looking for.

We are already free. No matter how much we seem to be conditioned or identified with our body, none of that ever touches us in actuality. In the same way as no thunderstorm has ever left a mark in the sky, we are never truly touched by *our* feelings or thoughts, although it might appear that way. We are already and always will be free. We do not have to do anything or go anywhere to become freer. This is not to deny, run away or hide from *negative* or *bad* feelings, but to fully embrace them and realize that our nature is different from them.

We give everything all the meaning it has. Life does not have any intrinsic meaning whatsoever. There is neither a given purpose nor an inherent passion that we have to find in the same way as we would search for Easter eggs. Whether we believe we are a victim of our life situation or childhood or the one controlling everything, it is us who give that meaning to life. From a young age on, we collect ideas and beliefs about the world and constantly gather evidence to validate those. If we collected other ideas, we would find evidence for those as well because there is evidence for every idea or belief out there. This is how our seeming reality is created every day. Our ideas or beliefs appear to be real to us and other ideas and beliefs appear to be real to others. There is no need to argue about who is right because everyone is always right and always has good enough evidence to back up their perspective on how they see the world.

Awareness brings about change. We do not have to follow any path, method or technique to discover truth. While following methods may be helpful to learn a new language, a music instrument or how to play tennis, it won't help us when it comes to understanding ourselves and leading a truly light-hearted, joyful and free life. We only seemingly need to use methods when being told we are lost and need something to hold on to. By becoming aware of certain mechanisms, we are able to naturally change things that were blind spots to us before. Becoming aware of who we are *not* is enough to bring about change. At the same time, it is essential that we are being aware right when or even before a given event takes place.

We are not in the world, but the world is in us. Since we are neither the body nor any other object, we are not in an objective world that can be found somewhere *out there*. The world, that is, the form, cannot exist independently of our awareness or consciousness, that is, the formless space that everything is made of. There is no object outside of or separate from consciousness. None of us has ever experienced anything without being aware of it.

Time only exists in the realm of thinking. In the moments, in which we are fully alive, that is, in the *now*, we are intuitively aware that time does not exist. We all know those moments, in which we do not think of the past or the future and completely *forget* about *our* worries. Alternatively, the more we think and live according to time, the less we feel at peace, in which case, it seems as if time had us in its grip. The existence of man-made time measurement devices is not proof enough for time to exist.

There is nothing but life. When there is only one entity, there is nothing to worry about and we can finally understand what it means to find true rest. Life according to this perspective is light-hearted and easy. There are no others that we have to impress, get approval from or report to. All there is is life playing with itself. Everything is an expression of the same. There is no privacy, nothing to be ashamed of and nothing to hide.

Life is perfect at any given moment. If we catch ourselves denying this statement, we find ourselves in a position, in which we compare an image of how the world is supposed to be according to our definition of being perfect with how we interpret the world based on what appears to us. This gap makes us believe that life is not perfect. Life won't be more complete when we reach ambitious goals or become a better person. Everything is perfect the way it is, whether we agree with it or not.

Now, this moment is crucial. You may notice thoughts such as *Of course, we are the thinker of our thoughts; who else would otherwise think them?* or *Of course I am an individual.* It would be easy to be guided by such thoughts and stop being open-minded. But it is essential to stay open even in such moments and truly see whether what you are reading is what may actually be happening, an assumption or just some non-sense. This is similar to when society was not able to accept Galileo's discovery of the earth not being flat and calling him *crazy*. Our first reaction to hearing unconventional statements is usually resistance and defense of the *current system*. It is usually easier for us to stay open-minded and listen to new possibilities when we have an intuition that what we hear could really be the case or when we struggle enough to realize the current way of living has never really served us.

It is neither about the destination nor the journey,
but about our essence that dwells
in this timeless moment.

62447015R00166

Made in the USA
Charleston, SC
15 October 2016